WITHDRAWN

WITHDRAWN

Great Survival Adventures

Exciting first-person accounts of men and women who found themselves in life-and-death situations—and managed to survive.

Great Survival Adventures

compiled and edited by
Robert Gannon

illustrated by Gil Cohen

RANDOM HOUSE 🏠 NEW YORK

Copyright © 1973 by Random House, Inc.
All rights reserved under International and Pan-American Copyright Conventions. Published in the United States by Random House, Inc., New York, and simultaneously in Canada by Random House of Canada Limited, Toronto.
Manufactured in the United States of America
Library of Congress Cataloging in Publication Data
Gannon, Robert.   Great survival adventures.
SUMMARY: A collection of true stories of survival against great odds recounted by the men and women who lived them.
1. Survival (after aeroplane accidents, shipwrecks, etc.)—Juvenile literature. [1. Survival] I. Cohen, Gil, illus. II. Title.
G525.G34   1973   904   73-3691
ISBN 0-394-82600-0   ISBN 0-394-92600-5 (lib. bdg.)

Acknowledgments

The publisher wishes to thank the following for permission to reprint copyrighted material:

CURTIS BROWN, LTD., for excerpts from *Hey, I'm Alive* by Helen Klaben with Beth Day, published by McGraw-Hill, Inc. Copyright © 1963, 1964 by Helen Klaben.

NICHOLAS B. CLINCH and his agent BLANCHE C. GREGORY, INC., for "We Scaled Doomsday Mountain." Reprinted from the Saturday Evening Post, March 25, 1961. Copyright © 1961 by Nicholas B. Clinch.

E. P. DUTTON & CO., INC., for material adapted from Chapter 13 of *Time Is Short and the Water Rises* by John Walsh with Robert Gannon. Copyright © 1967 by International Society for the Protection of Animals.

WILLIAM MORRIS AGENCY, INC., for "I Was Marooned on an Arctic Icecap." Reprinted from Colliers Magazine, December 13, 1952. Copyright 1952 by Colliers.

RANDOM HOUSE, INC., for "The Bloody Road to Usumbura," adapted from *Congo Kitabu* by Jean-Pierre Hallet. Copyright © 1965 by Jean-Pierre Hallet. Reprinted from True Magazine, May 1965 (Copyright © 1965, Fawcett Publications, Inc.).

THE READER'S DIGEST for "Trapped in the Desert," reprinted from the August 1964 Reader's Digest (Copyright © 1964 by the Reader's Digest Assn., Inc.); and for "Death and the Friendly River," reprinted from the January 1968 Reader's Digest (Copyright © 1968 by the Reader's Digest Assn., Inc.).

PAUL R. REYNOLDS, INC., for "We Rowed and Rowed . . . and Rowed—8000 Miles Across the Pacific." Copyright © 1972, 1973 by John Fairfax. Published by W. W. Norton & Company, Inc. Reprinted from True Magazine, August 1972 (Copyright © 1972 by Fawcett Publications, Inc.).

THE SATURDAY EVENING POST for "I Had to Bail Out at Supersonic Speed." Reprinted from the Saturday Evening Post, March 13, 1954. Copyright 1954 by the Curtis Publishing Company.

Contents

Introduction   8

1. Trapped in the Desert   12
   by Gary Beeman

2. Upstream Against the Rapids   24
   by John Walsh with Robert Gannon

3. Marooned on an Icecap   34
   by Charles W. Stover with Bill Davidson

4. The Bloody Road to Usumbura   52
   by Jean-Pierre Hallet

5. Death and the Friendly River 72
   by Scott Seegers

6. Doomsday Mountain 84
   by Nicholas B. Clinch

7. "We Rowed . . . and Rowed . . . and Rowed" 102
   by John Fairfax

8. Ordeal in the Yukon 120
   by Helen Klaben with Beth Day

9. Bail-Out at Supersonic Speed 138
   by Arthur Ray Hawkins with Wesley Price

Introduction

Adventures come in two distinct flavors. The first is the looked-for experience. You plan to climb a mountain or cross an ocean—and you know that before you're through you'll have a grand adventure whether you succeed or fail. The other kind is the unexpected, accidental event. You plan to row across a river to take some pictures and suddenly you find yourself being bounced from rock to rock in the icy current.

I'm an adventurer myself. As adventure editor of *Popular Science*, I have parachuted into the Atlantic on a survival experiment, flown through a hurricane, trained with the astronauts and done half a hundred other things most people only dream of.

But I know from my own experience that most people—even those who seek adventure—don't willingly put their own lives in danger. In the stories that follow, men and women of many different backgrounds suddenly are faced with the challenge of simply staying alive. They tell in their own words how they met that challenge. Braving injury, thirst, hunger, heat and cold, they managed to save their own lives and often the lives of others as well.

The authors of these stories found that when lives were at stake, they were a little smarter, a little stronger and a little braver than they ever dreamed was possible. Their accounts make exciting reading for all of us who wonder what we would do if we faced similar life-and-death situations.

ROBERT GANNON

Great Survival Adventures

Trapped in the Desert

BY GARY BEEMAN

1

You take a wrong turn and your car gets stuck in the sand. It's a bother, but nothing to worry about, really—unless you happen to be in the middle of California's Mojave Desert where temperatures sometimes reach 120 degrees, and you have only two pints of water between you . . .

• It began innocently enough, that hot June night in 1959, when I turned off U.S. 91 in the middle of the Mojave Desert and headed the old black coupe down a gravel road. I was only 18, and I didn't understand how a moment of thoughtlessness in the midsummer desert can lead you, step by irrevocable step, to disaster.

An aged prospector had told us—my 16-year-old school friend Jim Twomey and me—that the road led to derelict Rasor Ranch, on the edge of an area called the Devil's Playground. Desert "ghost settlements" fascinated me, and so did the prospector's report of rattlesnakes there. As a budding zoology major, I collected animal specimens to help pay for such wandering vacations as this.

We had a couple of days' food in the car, and there was supposed to be a good well at Rasor. Still, I'd never have turned off the highway with only two pints of water in our canteens if I hadn't been so tired. It was almost midnight. We'd driven more than 400 miles from San Francisco; then we'd bird-watched most of a sun-scorched afternoon.

Turning off the highway at a half-buried tire the prospector had told us about, I drove down the moonlit gravel road. After a long way—I didn't notice just *how* long—we hit a little finger of sand that had drifted across the road. I gunned the car, and we plowed over it, then over three more drifts.

After the fourth, our headlights showed no firm gravel road, only pale, undulating sand. For a few feet the car gained momentum. Then its spinning wheels began to dig down. We shuddered to a halt.

Obviously, I'd taken a wrong turn. We got out and paced the distance back to the road: 200 feet. Jim wanted to sleep and dig out next morning. "No," I said. "Let's get out now. It'll take only a few minutes."

An hour later, we hadn't moved an inch. The rear wheels had dug deeper, that was all. Then, searching for rocks in the moonlight, we stumbled onto the remains of an old railroad track. The steel had been salvaged, but a few ties remained. We found nine in various degrees of preservation.

Using one as a firm base, we jacked up the car and laid a double strip of ties, starting at the front wheels and extending out behind. Then I eased the car backward. It moved slowly but steadily: two feet—six feet—ten feet. Then one wheel slipped off a tie and the car stopped.

All through that long, frustrating night we jacked up the car, rearranged the ties, reversed a few feet until the inevitable slip. I figured we'd come at least 12 miles from the highway, perhaps 20. But what really mattered was that 200 feet of sand between the car and the gravel road. By five o'clock in the morning we'd covered perhaps 50 feet—still 150 to go. Exhausted, we drank all but two cupfuls of our water, then slept on the bare sand.

Almost at once, it seemed, the sun was beating fiercely down. Now, in stark daylight, things looked more serious. We could see why this sandbowl was called the Devil's Playground. Only scraggly bushes broke the barren, stony slopes. Ahead, a dry soda lake glared blindingly white.

Stripped to the waist, we went to work on the car. Within half an hour the sun was burning our skin. The sand soon grew too hot to touch. "Let's rest till evening," I suggested. "We'll get her out once it cools down." Jim didn't need much persuading. We decided we'd shelter in one of the rock faces of a hill that thrust up a quarter mile across the sand. I still wasn't really worried. In fact, before we left the car I shot a few feet of movie film.

We found two shady hideaways, 30 feet apart.

Sprawled under a shallow overhang, I dozed fitfully. The sunlight moved steadily closer, beating savagely up from the pale sand. Soon a bare foot of shade remained. My lips began to crack.

About noon we shared the last two cupfuls of water. Afterward, I lay and watched the line of sunlight, waiting for it to retreat. I kept wondering how hot it really was.

At last, a wedge of shade moved up unexpectedly from one side. The sun set; a wonderful coolness fell. Somewhere out in the desert, a whippoorwill began its plaintive song. Jim and I went down to the car and ate our first food in 24 hours—the first we'd wanted. We each finished a can of chicken noodle soup—preheated by the inferno inside the black coupe—then shared the juice from a small can of pineapple.

The food revived us, and we discussed whether to try walking out. Jim felt too weak for such a long trek, and I rated my own chances a bare 50–50. We decided to keep working on the car. I didn't really grasp, even then, that we were in desperate danger. I knew that unwary motorists had died of thirst in the desert; not long before, in Death Valley just 30 miles to the north, the dried-out corpses of two young men had been found close beside their stalled car. But somehow I felt it couldn't happen to us.

My memories of that second night are blurred. It was all we could do to jack up the car and run it back a few feet until it slipped off the disintegrating ties. We kept resting, I remember, and half-dozing. About four o'clock we fell asleep.

When I awoke, the half-risen sun was already burning my skin like an infrared lamp. Every movement demanded effort. And now for the first time I understood our peril: During the night we had moved the car barely 15 feet; more than 130 feet remained! Jim, weak and listless, seemed to have lost hope. With rocks and twigs I laid out a four-foot S.O.S.; then we started toward our rock shelters.

Right from the start, that second day was terrible. Even in my shady overhang, I could feel the heat sucking moisture out of my body. And it wasn't only the heat. The silence was almost as bad. I found myself straining for sounds, but all I could hear was my heartbeat. The drumbeat inside me swamped everything.

Occasionally I'd hear Jim's heavy breathing. Then he began to babble, in dream or delirium. "What about my grape drink?" he kept saying. "I've paid for it, and I want my grape drink." At last he fell silent.

Soon, the noonday sun was pressing my strip of shade tight against the overhang. Once, I heard the lisp of sifting sand. Four feet away a rattlesnake was moving past, from shade to shade.

I lay in a daze now, never quite dozing, never fully awake. I had given up hope that the day would ever pass its peak. Once, when I squinted out at the car, shimmering in the heat haze a quarter mile away, there was another car parked beside our coupe—and a stream of vehicles rushing up and down the black highway on which they stood. Had I, after all, walked out to the highway? I twisted my head; then squinted out again; the old black coupe stood on pale sand, alone.

Panic swept me. I knew dehydration eventually unbalances your mind. If I could already see a nonexistent highway, had I been *acting* irrationally?

At last, in midafternoon, I could stand the terrible dryness no longer. Struggling to my feet, I went out into the sun. When I looked down toward the car, I saw for the first time that the flat sand near it had once been a lake. "If I dig," I thought, "perhaps I'll find water." I staggered down the hill.

There were green-leaved creosote bushes growing on a small sand dune, and I remembered that when digging for lizards in such places I had found moisture. I began digging into the side of the dune, in among the bushes' roots. There was no water; but suddenly I realized that my hands felt almost cool. Perhaps I could dig a cave and crawl into that wonderful coolness!

I don't know how long it took me to scoop out a hole. But at last it was big enough. I stripped off all my sweat-grimed clothes and crawled in. The cool sand soothed me like a balm. I fell asleep.

I woke to see the sun sinking below a line of hills. The plaintive whistle of my whippoorwill came at last. I felt cool and rested. Then, without warning, Jim staggered past. His head lolled; his arms hung loose at his sides. Suddenly he sank to one knee, then pitched forward and lay still. I shook him. He moaned faintly.

Alarmed, I hurried to the car and searched feverishly through the inferno inside it. Under the seat I found a bottle of aftershave lotion. I wrenched off the top and put it to my lips. The shock of what tasted like hot rubbing alcohol brought me up short. Again I had that horrible, fleeting comprehension of my unhinged state of mind.

I began rubbing lotion on my face and neck. It felt good. So I went back to Jim, rubbed lotion on his face and poured it over his T-shirt. He was deathly pale, his mouth hung open, and dried mucus flecked his scaly white lips. "We need a drink," I kept thinking. "We both need a drink."

Desperately, I ran my eyes over the car. And suddenly I was thinking, *"The radiator!"* I'd always known that in the desert your radiator water could save you; yet for two days I'd ignored it! I grabbed a saucepan, squirmed under the front bumper and unscrewed the radiator drainage tap. A stream of rust-brown water poured down over the greasy sway bar and splashed into my saucepan. It was the most wonderful sight I had ever seen.

Still lying under the car, I took several huge gulps. The water was thick with oil and rust. Almost at once, though, I began to feel better. When I had drained the radiator and filled a canteen, I went back to Jim and poured water into his open mouth. He stirred.

Then I returned to the car, got a can of chow mein and ate half of it. Soon Jim was sitting up and eating his half of the chow mein.

My mind felt clearer, and I realized that if we were to get out I'd have to try something new. After a while I saw what would have been obvious if I had been thinking clearly: that I would have to run the car back off the ties at high speed and just hope I could keep it going.

We were still pitifully weak. When Jim tried to help he collapsed over the jack, and the rest of that third night he lay prostrate. I must have spent five or six hours over a job that would normally take 20 minutes: aligning the car perfectly on the ties for our final attempt. I knew that if we failed the first time I wouldn't have the strength to try again. At last, utterly exhausted, I fell asleep.

I awoke in hot sunlight. Hurriedly, we drank the last of the water. I helped Jim into the car, started the motor, and let it idle for a few moments. Then I looked at Jim, sprawled across the seat. "This is it," I said. He didn't seem to hear.

I revved the motor, slammed the automatic transmission into reverse and stamped on the accelerator. The car leaped backward. It gained speed, slipped off the ties . . . kept going. All at once, a tie banged hard, somewhere up front. The car faltered, almost stopped. Then the tie snapped, and we were moving again.

But soon we were slowing down. The rear wheels started to dig in with a horribly familiar sinking motion. They would spin, grip for a moment, then spin again. And, all the time, the motor was slowing down, the car sinking into the sand. We'd almost stopped when I felt the tires grab something solid. They spun again . . . grabbed and spun . . . grabbed. For interminable moments we hung poised between life and death. Then the tires took firm grip and we were moving smoothly. At last we were out on the gravel road, and I was whooping like an idiot. Beside me, Jim was smiling weakly.

Four hours later, after many sweltering halts for the now-dry motor to cool, we turned onto the highway; we'd been stuck only six miles off U.S. 91. And within another mile—less than seven from the desolate sand-bowl where we'd faced a terrible death—we came to a modern roadside cafe.

"Kinda warm today, boys," the man behind the counter said. Then he took another look at us and saw that we were drained dry, caked with grime and dead-tired.

He put two glasses of water on the counter. "Just sip it a little, boys," he said, "until you get used to it."

Upstream Against the Rapids

BY JOHN WALSH WITH ROBERT GANNON

2

A few years ago a great dam was built in the South American country of Surinam. It stretched across the huge Surinam River, and behind it eventually grew a lake 870 square miles. The people who lived in the flooded territory were called Saramaccas. They were descendants of rebellious African slaves brought to the country some three centuries ago.

The land behind the dam was hilly, and as the water rose, each hill became a gradually shrinking island. The Surinam government transported the people to safe ground, but the jungle animals were left behind.

Then officials of the ISPA (International Society for the Protection of Animals) heard about it and sent down John Walsh, a young man trained in rescue techniques by the Massachusetts SPCA. He lived with the Saramaccas in the rain forest for 18 dramatic months in a danger-filled struggle to save the animals. By the time he returned to the States he had rescued nearly 10,000 of them.

In the following account, he tells of a hair-raising trip up the Surinam River in a native-built dugout boat pushed by an outboard motor.

- While most of the time in any situation I was the boss, during a run through river rapids I had nothing whatever to do but sit in the center of the dugout and hold on, like any tourist. Let me try to help whoever was navigating by offering suggestions or steering with a paddle, and he would yell at me as though I were a naughty kid.

But I really wanted to see what would happen if I tried it alone. So one day I wrapped a Mae West around me, put another around the boat motor, and set off in the most maneuverable dugout we had. I had been whizzing around the lake for any number of months now, and thought I was getting to be a pretty good seaman.

So I tried it, tried going upstream in a typically fast current through a few relatively minor rapids.

In the space of maybe ten minutes I came to a rather surprising conclusion: I can't run a dugout with a motor worth a damn. Further, I doubt that I could ever learn. I couldn't navigate even the first fast-flowing current between the rocks without banging the side of the boat, running over boulders, clanging the propeller blade. I tried simply to hold the boat steady in the current, and couldn't even do that. The dugout would start swaying, sweep wider and wider until the nose no longer could hold its upriver point, and then slide sidewise. The boat would smack a rock broadside and nearly go over.

I gave it one last try, gunning up the fast current maybe 50 feet or so, and *ping!* there went the prop.

The current hair-raisingly swept me the 50 feet back down to calm water. Dejectedly I headed back to camp.

Because of this experience I especially appreciated the skill of the men a week later when we ran the rapids at night. I wanted to go upriver, to the little Saramaccan settlement of Biakoetoe to talk to the village captain. He had ordered two of my best men back home to work on one of his projects, and I needed them myself.

In the back of the boat, running the motor, was Llo Drak. He was a rather urbane Saramacca with a walrus moustache and an immense front gold tooth, which he revealed often. He always wore a Great White Hunter's pith helmet, and he had two wives in two upriver villages. He had built their homes and cleared farming *grons* for them, and they in turn did the farmwork and kept the huts spotless.

Guiding in front was Wolf Wachter, 39—older than most of my men—very calm and serious. He had a fine, kind face, usually equipped with a shy half-smile. His eyes looked tired, the whites were yellow, and he wasn't very good at spotting animals in the trees. I figured his sight was failing.

We got a late start that day, and by the time we chugged up the first series of rapids, it was late afternoon. We couldn't make the worst of the rapids before nightfall, I saw—some ten miles of them lay ahead of us—so I planned to spend the night in a little village on the shore. But Llo and Wolf, who had been talking together in low tones earlier, recommended that we go ahead. The sky was clear and the moon full, they pointed out. Well, if they wanted to chance it, okay with me.

(The next day I found out why they pressed to go ahead. It was Llo. He hadn't seen one of his wives in some weeks, and he wanted to get upstream to be with her that night.)

In the clean, nearly equatorial thin air of Surinam, the moon shines with a brilliance unknown in the States. The forest had an eerie quality that night, but the seeing was superb, and when we'd pass through a rapids section, motor roaring and boat tilting up at an angle, the splashing water shined as though phosphorescent.

Then trouble. First the sky clouded. And then the motor started coughing from fuel-line cloggings. We pulled to shore, cleaned out the offending tubes, filters, and bowl, and put things back together again. By then the moon was covered. We dug through our supplies and Wolf came up with a flashlight—perhaps the worst one this side of Cayenne. It glowed with the intensity of maybe two candlepower, barely illuminating the water a half-dozen feet in front of us and the occasional ruby eyes of a caiman.

We set out again, led by that absurd flashlight, and now I began to get apprehensive. I noticed that Wolf and Llo had stopped bantering and joking; now it was strictly business. Wolf, on his knees in the front, would shine the flashlight ahead, then to the sides, then hold it upright and move it one way or the other, signaling Llo to go to the sides, straight ahead, faster, slower.

Suddenly lightning ripped the sky apart and rain poured down in torrents. We slid into plastic raincoats. The night was solid black now, and Wolf's flashlight lit nothing but the streaming rain a foot or two in front of it. Its only function was to direct Llo. The savior was the lightning; it would flash and the men would get their bearings and I would shudder as I'd see rocks and rapids and five-foot, midriver waterfalls around us.

Wolf, I found out later, was going by sound almost as much as sight. Lightning would light up the path before us, showing the safe spots and the rocks, then for the next 50 feet we'd move in complete blackness, with only the crashing of water to guide him. Then the lightning would flash again, he'd signal Llo a direction adjustment, and we'd travel on.

When I looked up and forward into the rain, I could see nothing at all. I felt as though I were staring into a shower spigot. Once I glanced up at Wolf and saw him frantically motioning with the light to go forward. Against the sound of the motor and the rain and the rapids I could hear him yell, *"Esi! esi! esi!"* (Fast! Fast! Fast!"). Llo turned the motor full, and the boat lunged forward, tilted sharply, fighting against the inclined plane of current flowing down a trough in the rocks. I'd never again accuse Wolf of having poor eyesight.

Suddenly things were relatively quiet; the rapids noise had gone, the rain had changed to a pitter-patter, and the engine sounded oddly muffled, as though we were going through a cavern. Actually we were. We were passing down a creek leading from one great arm of the Surinam to the other, through a tunnel of leaves and vines and brush. We had to lean forward to keep from being whacked by hanging greenery.

The tunnel was perhaps 500 feet long, and up ahead I could hear more rapids, louder and louder. "That's a mean one," Wolf said in Saramaccan, now that his voice could be heard again. "The last big one; but if we tip over there, all our bones will break."

We entered the river again, swerved swiftly upstream, then across, then up again, back, and then Wolf signaled forward again. The boat tilted to slide up a grade. The roar of the rain suddenly was drowned out by the more intense crash of rushing water.

And then the nauseating crunch of wood against rock as the side of the dugout struck a boulder. The boat lurched, swung sideways, and *clink!* the propeller hit a rock. The motor stopped—suddenly, unexpectedly, horrifyingly. The world came to a halt as the dugout stopped its forward motion, paused, then began to move back, then to rush sickeningly down the rapids in the dark.

Without the motor, our control was virtually zero. Wolf had a pole and Llo had a paddle, but rushing through the rapids they were nearly useless. "When we go over, hang onto the boat!" Wolf screamed in my ear. I was trying to decide what I should try to save—my camera or bag of survival gear or sleeping hammock. Conclusion: me. Forget the rest.

The dugout struck a rock with its stern, swung us around sideways while the men strove to turn it parallel to the current again. But before they could, we struck a boulder broadside. The boat tipped and water washed over the side, filling it to our shins. I grabbed a calabash and started splashing water out, glad I could do something. The boat slipped off the rock and started down again, while Wolf and Llo shouted at each other in Saramaccan so rapidly I couldn't follow.

Suddenly Wolf lunged, grabbed upward, out in the night, and somehow caught a branch. He was lifted up and out, but he hooked his toes under the boat seat. I jumped up and grabbed his legs, and the boat swung around and smacked against the rocks by the shore as more water poured in. Llo leaped out, snatched a tie rope and looped it around a tree, as Wolf and I, then with Llo, using calabash dishes, frantically bailed water. We gained on it, and gradually the level inside the boat dropped.

And then the three of us simply stood there on the shore, panting, while the boat snugged thumping against the rocks.

By the aid of the firefly flashlight we inspected the motor, found it undamaged; the shock of hitting the rock simply had jarred it to a stop. One pull and it roared to life. But Llo shut it off. We'd walk the boat up this part of the rapids.

The rough water stretched for only 60 yards, but it felt like a thousand. Though rain continued to pour in the blackness, it barely could be heard above the cata-

ract thundering beside us. The flashlight, useless, was put away, and the only light came from the occasional lightning. The rocks were slippery, and first one, then another of us, slipped and fell, skinning our knees and banging our arms, and falling into the churning water almost to be swept downstream. Twice one of us went down and dragged the other two along, almost losing the boat.

But we did make it up to the rapids head, to relatively calm water where we could again use the motor in comparative safety. And wouldn't you know, during the last two- or three-mile section of child-size rapids, broken by long stretches of calm water, the rain stopped and the moon came out.

As we chugged up to the landing at Biakoetoe, glorying in the full moon, I dug through my water-drenched supplies and came up with a third-full bottle of rum. We each had a healthy gulp—after first spilling a little on one side of the boat, then on the other, as is the custom, to thank Apucuu, the river spirit, for allowing us to go through the rapids safely.

And for good measure, after we had drunk—and with the obvious agreement of Wolf and Llo—I turned the bottle bottom up and gave the river the rest.

Marooned on an Icecap

BY CHARLES W. STOVER WITH BILL DAVIDSON

3

At 20 degrees below zero, with two ribs and two vertebrae fractured, trapped in a snow desert five times the size of France and 500 miles from rescue, how do you cope? You rely on your amazingly resilient human body—and your fellow human beings. "I saw man's best instincts come to the fore," says the author. "Those eight days I was lost in the ice age comprise the greatest experience of my life."

• Think of a time machine transporting a party of explorers back one million years to the ice age, and you will have some idea of what happened to me on a September morning not so long ago.

We were on a supply run, bringing building materials for a new scientific base high atop the Greenland Icecap, and I was checking cargo in the cabin of our British Hastings four-engine transport. The pilot, Flight Lieutenant Michael Clancy, a rotund, 34-year-old Irishman, was flying low while the rest of us pushed out supplies.

Suddenly I heard a rending, grinding noise, and I was thrown against the front wall of the cabin. I hung there for an instant, and then I was hurled the length of the cabin to the *rear* wall, banging against flying gasoline cans and my plane mates as I sailed by. The moment of chaos was followed by an awful silence. The plane was down!

I heard someone scream, "Let's get out of here before it catches fire!"—and I tumbled out into the snow. One of the crew members was lying there, his face covered with blood. We didn't know whether he was alive or dead, but we dragged him 50 feet, out of range of the explosive gasoline which flooded the area from spring tanks. It was only then that I realized the mess we were in.

It was 20 degrees below zero and getting colder. We were in the center of the 800-mile-wide, 1,500-mile-long icecap at a point where the cap rose more than a mile and a half into the air. No one had ever been able to live on this foreboding remnant of the ice age except a handful of hardy scientific pioneers. Not only that, but to my knowledge no aircraft had ever been able to land and take off in the rarefied atmosphere of this 8,000-foot-high desert of snow.

But our biggest problem was immediate. Unless we got our emergency survival equipment out of the crashed plane, we wouldn't even live through the night.

What had happened those few minutes ago, we figured out later, was that Clancy, up in the cockpit, had experienced an arctic phenomenon known as the "white-out," in which a mist blots out the horizon and the white sky blends completely with the white ice surface in a swirl of blowing snow. When that happens, you can't tell where one ends and the other begins. Clancy didn't have any idea he was only 20 feet above the ice as he lowered the left wing to wheel the plane for a pass at the drop area. The left wing ripped into the snowy surface at about 145 miles per hour.

Only superb piloting by Clancy prevented us from flipping over and being smashed to bits. As it was, he just managed to wrestle the right wing down, and the plane slid into a complete turn on its belly, grinding to a stop facing in the opposite direction. The two port engines were torn off, and the left wing was crumpled, but miraculously the cabin remained intact.

This was the sight we were staring at moments later when we heard a terrifying cry: "The number three engine is on fire!"

We knew if the plane burned with our sleeping bags and other emergency equipment, we would be without shelter and the cold could kill us within a few hours. So we sprang to the burning engine, dousing it with every piece of fire-fighting equipment we could lay our hands on. The fire sputtered and died before it could spread to the hundreds of gallons of high-test gasoline seeping from the plane.

But our troubles were just beginning.

As soon as the fire was out we assessed the extent of our injuries. We were all hurt to some degree. But the

only serious casualty appeared to be the radio operator, Frank Burke. It was his unconscious body we had dragged away from the plane right after the crash. Burke had deep cuts in the scalp and face, and was suffering from concussion. We covered him as best we could to keep him from freezing to death. Then, presumably because we were all in a state of shock, we milled aimlessly about, making silly remarks to one another. I recall saying to Clancy, "Do you always land aircraft this way?"

Shortly we looked up and saw a dog sled approaching. It was Commander C. J. W. Simpson, head of the scientific encampment, and two of his party, rushing over from their tiny camp a mile or so away. Their arrival jolted us into a full realization of our predicament. We suddenly realized that their lives, as well as ours, were at stake.

In order to lighten their load for the difficult ascent onto the icecap, the Simpson people had stripped their equipment to the barest essentials, taking with them only two tents, their sleds and 26 ounces of rations per man per day. They and their dogs had reached North-Ice exhausted, weak with fatigue and hunger. They had taken the calculated risk of depending on our air drop for every item of food, shelter and clothing necessary to keep them alive when they arrived at their site on the icecap. Yet, the air drop hadn't even really begun, and here we were, 12 battered men for Simpson's six-man party to worry about in their own weakened and dangerously ill-equipped state.

Commander Simpson dressed Burke's wounds, and then we held a council of war. We decided that the fuselage of the plane provided the only possible shelter in the open, driftless waste, and that we'd all have to live in it. Simpson also decided to move his two-tent camp over to the wrecked plane to shorten our lines of communication.

Then, slowly, the commander began to discuss our chances of getting out.

There was no thought of air rescue, which he believed to be impossible. "In a few weeks," he said, "we'll take you out to the east coast by dog sled. It'll be a rugged 300-mile trip, so you'd better prepare yourselves for it. It'll be twenty-five or thirty days of the toughest traveling you'll ever have to face. It'll be in the period of 24-hour total darkness, and we'll have to pick our way over a 75-mile-wide area crisscrossed with bottomless crevasses. We nearly lost a man in one of them in broad daylight on the way up here."

With these thoughts to chew on, we began to prepare our shelter for the night, moving all the cargo out of the fuselage of the wrecked plane and arranging the cabin into one small cooking compartment and one large sleeping section. Clancy and I took stock of the supplies. We found that we had rations for 10 days, and not nearly enough arctic clothing to go around.

We seemed fairly well off for the time being—but in the midst of the inventory taking, Donald Barker-Simson, the loadmaster, suddenly sat down. "I can't walk," he said. "There's something wrong with my ankle." (It was broken.) About an hour later I began to feel stiffness and sharp pains in my chest and back. Soon, I could do nothing but sit down alongside Barker-Simson. (I had fractured two ribs and two vertebrae.) We both just leaned back on a pile of gear, suffering excruciating pain.

In a matter of minutes, our difficulties had trebled. We now had three serious casualties instead of one—which made a 300-mile overland trip seem even more forbidding.

When the shock of our latest misfortune wore off, the nine able-bodied survivors continued to prepare our quarters. No sooner had they set up one of our two tiny emergency stoves in the rear of the plane than they had a pot of tea brewing.

We went to bed when it got dark, at about four o'clock that afternoon. We three casualties were placed in our sleeping bags fully clothed, and Clancy made us as comfortable as possible on excelsior padding, where we were to lie for the duration of the ordeal.

We could not light a stove in this section because it was too close to the gasoline fumes seeping from the sprung tanks in the wings. I have never been so cold in my life. The temperature outside had dropped to about 30 degrees below zero. In the cabin it was about 15 below, and the 8,000-foot-thick ice just a few inches below me seemed to be jabbing a thousand icicles into my back.

I was comforted by only one thought. Commander Simpson's radio operator had managed to get a message through to Thule, using our aircraft's radio. I guessed that the news of the crash soon would reach the outside world, and that my wife, Marjorie, in Portland, Maine, would at least know I was still alive.

I must have dozed a bit toward morning on Wednesday, our second day on the icecap, because the next thing I knew I was surrounded by the entire party singing, "Happy birthday, dear Smokey, happy birthday to you." It was indeed my birthday—my thirty-fifth.

But this brief ceremony was only an interlude in another day of hardship. I looked up and noticed that two inches of frost had formed on the inside of the plane. Clancy noticed it, too. He whistled and said, "Men, unless you want to sleep in an ice cave, you've got some work to do." So they spent the rest of the day rounding up the parachutes with which we had dropped the heavier supplies the day before. Then they strung a network of parachute cords all over the cabin, draping them with layer after layer of silk.

By nightfall we had two rather exotic-looking compartments about $5\frac{1}{2}$ feet high, 7 feet wide and 15 feet long. The idea was to cut down the space with insulated silk walls that would better retain body heat. Actually, it didn't work very well, but it had an interesting psychological effect. We thought it was working, so we all felt better.

Shortly after noon on Wednesday I heard Simpson's radio operator yell, "Hey, another Hastings is looking for us," and sure enough, ten minutes later the plane was overhead. Captain Oswald Wetzel, Jr., of Shreveport, Louisiana, the provost marshal at Thule, was aboard, and I could hear him shouting over the plane's radio, "How are you, Smokey? How serious are your injuries?" I couldn't move from my sleeping bag, but I told him as best I could, relaying my answers through the radioman.

It was quite a wrench hearing the voice of an old friend, so near and yet so far. When he left I was swept by the most depressing feeling of loneliness. In addition, my pain grew progressively worse, and I developed a cough (which later turned out to be pneumonia). Now the "icicles" were jabbing into my chest as well as my back, and I was tempted to ask for morphine. But I knew that morphine might deaden all pain to the extent that I might unknowingly allow my hands or feet to become frostbitten. So I fought off the impulse.

Then I tried to eat, but couldn't. It was the same menu kept on the stove three times a day—bacon, stew, hard bread and tea. But if it had been sirloin steak, I couldn't have downed it. The rest of the night was another ordeal of sleeplessness for Burke, Barker-Simson and me.

Thursday, our third day on the icecap, was eventful. First, Captain Wetzel flew back and dropped boots, parkas, sleeping bags, an aircraft heater (which was smashed in the drop), a bottle of whisky (which did *not* smash) and—wonder of wonders—mail.

Meantime, radio-operator Kenneth Taylor, as a result of superhuman effort, had kept the generators going and was in radio contact with home base. He was working 15 hours a day, sometimes with bare hands in the bitter cold. As he walked past my sleeping bag for that afternoon's broadcast, I noticed his hands were a mass of frostbite blisters. "Don't worry," he said, "I can still work the key with my knuckles. Besides, my hands aren't too bad. It's just the skin."

That night, I had a chance to emulate Taylor's stoicism. The doctor back at base had prescribed treatment for me, and now the men began to carry it out. First, while we temporarily disregarded the risk of fire, all available lamps and stoves were brought into the sleeping compartment. The concentration of heat raised the interior temperature from 39 degrees below zero to about 10 below zero. Then, with three men propping me up, two others stripped off my four layers of clothes. My skin turned blue with cold in a matter of seconds, but the men rubbed my bare body while someone deftly strapped adhesive plaster around my torso. The entire treatment took no more than 15 minutes, but I didn't recover from the added pain of it for days. That night, for the first and only time, I asked for morphine—and I think I slept.

The next morning, Friday, I ate my first food. The mess-gear was caked with the residue of a dozen previous meals because we had no hot water for washing. By this time, the men who had not been badly injured found that exercise made them feel comparatively warm, and they spent most of the 12 daylight hours retrieving the air-drop packages and helping dig an excavation for the below-surface houses of the camp-to-be.

Throughout that day, Clancy seemed more than usually perturbed by our plight, and he made several comments indicating he felt personally guilty for it. Then an inspiration struck him, and he came over to where I lay and said, "Me boy, we're goin' to have a little feast tonight." I asked him what he meant and he said that our group and Simpson's had arranged to consolidate our food for the evening. "Also, we're goin' to have a little drink of angel's breath"—which is what he called whisky. In short, with our lives at stake in the middle of nowhere, we were going to have a party.

It was a great party. All 18 of us crowded into the limited space of the parachute-draped compartment where we three casualties lay. We sang and told stories and drank hot toddies made with melted snow.

Our good spirits continued into the next day, Saturday, our fifth on the icecap, because this was the day our hopes of rescue first soared. The plane came over at noon with an air drop, and in the midst of the radio discussion, Taylor yelled, "Hey, I've got contact with another plane—a rescue B-17!" We couldn't see it, but a moment later I was speaking with Major Donald Bussey, of San Bernardino, California, a friend from Thule.

"How you gettin' along, Smoke?" he asked.

"Fine," I lied.

"Is it possible to land some kind of aircraft there?"

I said, "What I've seen of it, I think it's favorable for a C-47 on skis."

He said, "Maybe we'll try tomorrow or the next day. Could you outline a runway and set off smoke pots to indicate wind direction? And when the rescue plane circles the area, could you have someone drive a dog sled down the runway in the direction you want us to land?"

With that, the contact faded, but Bussey's words left us nearly beside ourselves with joy.

The following day—Sunday—Commander Simpson came in to see me and said, "What's your religion, Smokey?" I told him I was a Protestant, and he asked, "Would you care to join us in an evening religious service?" I said sure, and didn't think any more about it. But that night, from the moment the men filed into the cabin, the spiritual impact of the ceremony hit me like a rock.

We had two tiny kerosene lamps, the pale-yellow light of which flickered against the multicolored silk of the parachute draperies. The bearded, dirty men sat and bared their heads. I have been in the world's greatest cathedrals, but I have never known—I have never felt—a more churchly atmosphere. Here we were in a beat-up, wrecked aircraft, hundreds of miles from nowhere. We had three religions represented, but we all faced the same isolation, the same problems, the same dangers, and we joined in common worship.

Sunday night I suffered more pain than ever before,

and if it hadn't been for the spiritual uplift of the afternoon ceremony, I don't think I could have borne it. The same was true of Monday, our seventh day on the icecap—our day of despair. From morning until night we waited for a radio signal, the sound of a plane's engine—anything to let us know that rescuers were on the way. But nothing happened. That black Monday was one of the lowest points of my life.

But all the despair vanished at 8:00 A.M. the next morning, Tuesday, September 23rd—the eighth day. Taylor came out of the radio compartment with a big grin on his face. "Well," he said, "they're coming. A Yank SA-16 is giving it a shot today, to try to take out the three injured." Heart-pounding excitement swept through the cabin at this news, but I tempered my optimism with the realization that the Air Rescue Service's Grumman SA-16 had never been able to take off or land successfully at these altitudes. I didn't say anything to the other men, however, and they swept outside jabbering, listening for the first sounds of the engines.

At 10:23 A.M. they heard the SA-16 approaching. Inside the cabin, we could just lie there. Clancy stationed his men with smoke pots around a level section of the icecap, and Commander Simpson drove his dog sled down the runway.

There was a breath-taking moment of silence, and then I heard a cheer go up from the men outside. The flying boat had put down—slithering along on the belly of its hull to a perfect landing. I was bundled onto a stretcher and hustled over to the plane—along with Burke and Barker-Simson.

But we were still a long way from safety. In order to develop enough power, the SA-16 had to be fitted with two JATO (jet-assisted take-off) units. Each weighed 200 pounds, and they had to be wrestled onto racks on either side of the fuselage. The SA-16's pilot, Major H. S. Julin, of Table Rock, Nebraska, didn't dare shut off his engines lest he couldn't start them again. So his crew and the Clancy-Simpson parties had to work in the unbelievable 60-degree-below-zero cold of the prop blast. Some developed frostbite; others dropped from altitude exhaustion. But somehow, after an hour of struggle, the JATO bottles were fastened in place.

Then the pilot opened the throttles wide. But the plane didn't move! The warm hull had melted the surface, which had frozen again. We were locked firmly into the icecap.

The SA-16's crew chief tumbled out and organized the ground party into two groups—one under each wing—to rock the plane until it broke loose. But in the ten seconds it took the crew chief to scramble back into the plane, the hull had frozen in again. By this time, however, Clancy had caught the idea. He and his men rocked us loose again.

The SA-16 made a take-off run—and my heart sank; I realized it was lumbering along at only about 30 miles per hour in the oxygen-thin air, less than half its minimum take-off speed. I had visions of four *more* men—the SA-16 crew—being added to our overland trek party.

Then Major Julin swung into another take-off run. We felt the bumping of the icecap beneath the hull, then the hissing of the JATO units as they exploded, and suddenly there was no more bumping. We were in the air.

Our ordeal was almost, but not quite, over. First, the heater went out in the plane, and to save Barker-Simson's frostbitten feet, the medic had to hold them under his own parka, against the warm, bare skin of his stomach, for the entire three hours of flight. Then we had to race a blizzard that was converging on Thule. We reached the air base with only 30 minutes of fuel left in our tanks. Five minutes later the field closed in for the day.

I never thought I'd be happy to see the ugly aluminum buildings of the remote outpost, but that afternoon, as I was unloaded from the SA-16 and rushed to the hospital, they looked like the skyline of New York.

The Bloody Road to Usumbura

BY JEAN-PIERRE HALLET

4

This story sounds more like fiction than fact. A man in the wilds of Burundi accidentally blows off his right hand with a charge of dynamite. Then, with blood spurting through the tourniquet, he drives over winding, tortuous African roads to the nearest hospital—200 miles away. And nobody along the whole route will help him.

• The small yellow flame licked at the one-foot length of Bickford fuse cord attached to the two sticks of dynamite I held in my right hand. I waited for the spark and the little crackling noise that would come when the fuse caught, but nothing happened. Two or three seconds passed as I held the flame of my lighter to the end of the fuse . . .

It was shortly before three o'clock in the afternoon. I was standing in a dugout canoe about 300 feet off the eastern shore of Lake Tanganyika, at the southern border of Burundi. Three other canoes were positioned in a crude circle around me, about 100 feet away. Each of them held two Bagoma fishermen who were waiting, nets in hand, for me to drop the charge into the water. The dynamite would sink slowly and explode at a depth of 15 feet. Then a cloud of stunned silvery fish would float up to the surface, and my helpers would scoop them into their nets.

Two or three seconds passed. Then, instead of a spark, there was a rapid, abnormal hiss-s-s-s-s. Something was wrong and I knew it. Immediately I started to toss the dynamite into the lake, but I was too late. The 200-gram charge went off in my right hand.

Seconds later, when awareness returned, I found myself in the cold blue immensity of Africa's deepest lake, gasping for breath as I instinctively treaded water. I was half blind and almost completely deaf from the blast. My face, neck and chest were laid open, my left hand was terribly wounded, and my right hand—I no longer had a right hand, only an abbreviated stub of an arm that ended just above the wrist in two jagged bones and some tattered frills of skin.

My canoe was still floating about 20 feet away—upside down. I looked for the other boats and saw, with a feeling of rage, that the native fishermen were paddling furiously toward the shore. Frightened by the prospect of being involved in a white man's death, my helpers were deserting me. Then I looked in the opposite direction and saw four greenish-gray snouts about 100 feet in the distance—crocodiles. They moved to-

ward me rapidly, with their ridged, scaly backs carving a wrinkled wake through the water . . .

It began less than a week before, in Bururi, where I loaded my pickup with axes and machetes, a 50-foot roll of fuse cord, detonators and a massive wooden box containing 50 sticks of dynamite, then set off for the lake to the west. The Mosso, an area about 60 miles from the lake, was in a devastating drought, and the people had virtually nothing to eat. It was my idea to help by dynamiting fish—a strictly illegal practice, but one that might keep a few people from starving.

Getting to the lake was tougher than I had thought. The trail was so overgrown that I had to break out the axes and machetes and send my helpers ahead to cut back the bush. Slowly, as they slashed a passage, my pickup and I crawled forward. Finally, after about three miles, we entered a dense growth of sizable trees. It was impossible to force our homemade highway any farther.

We hacked our way another mile along a small footpath until we reached the beach of Mwekarago Cove, a curved expanse of white sand almost completely overgrown with creeping lianas. Our fishermen, in boats, had already arrived. Then, while most of my native helpers watched from a respectful distance, I prepared my charges and paddled out from shore to fire the first blast. It worked. I filled the boat with fish, returned to shore, unloaded, and paddled back for the second. By the end of the first day, my truck was crammed with

2,500 pounds of shining, silvery fish.

It had been a terribly hard and exhausting day, but it was worth it. I shall never forget the expressions on the faces of those weak, emaciated people when they saw me arrive at Butana with the truckload of fish. They were successively astonished, unbelieving and incredibly happy.

During the next two days, I sped up the tempo, conducting both morning and afternoon blasting sessions at the cove, each followed by the long trip to Butana.

Now on the fourth day I had only six sticks of dynamite left from the original 50. I'd use them this afternoon, and the great "Fish Safari" would come to a quiet, successful end.

I touched the flame of my lighter to that last fuse. Then, suddenly, inexplicably, I found myself dazed and gasping for breath while my feet treaded water and my thoughts whirled in confusion.

Desperately, I tried to rub my eyes with the back of my right hand, but for some reason I couldn't manage to do it. I tried again and felt something sharp rake over my eyebrows. Something sharp? I ducked my head, hoping the water might bring back my vision. The maneuver worked, washing away the blood from my left eye. The right eye was apparently blind. I felt immense relief being able to see again. I raised my right arm out of the water.

For an instant I stared at the stump without comprehension. There was no blood; the white, macerated flesh looked like the skin of a plucked chicken. Abruptly I realized what I was looking at.

Now I began to feel pain, a terrible burning pain that raged over my face, neck, chest, arms and hands. My *hands?* The right one was still full of fire, despite the fact that it no longer existed. The pain in the left was even more frightful—if I still had it. That thought really shocked me. I raised my left arm out of the water—and the hand was still there. The thumb and the first two fingers were badly injured; they were split open like burst sausages, and the bones of my forefinger gleamed whitely through the torn skin. But the hand was still there.

Another thought came, and I reached down with my mangled fingers to pass them over my belly, half expecting to find coils of dangling intestine. Nothing seemed to be wrong. Instinctively I explored a little farther down. Undamaged.

Then I looked again at the stump of my right arm. Only a few seconds before, the severed wrist had been dead white in color. Now it was spurting jets of bright red arterial blood. I flexed the limb as hard as I could and pressed the inner surface against the upper part of my chest, squeezing the arteries. That slowed the stream to a trickle.

Then, for the first time, I looked around me and saw the native fishermen paddling off into the distance and the white wakes of water made by the oncoming crocodiles.

That sight shocked me into action. I struck out toward the land with an awkward, left-handed Australian crawl, keeping my right arm pressed against my ribs. The pain was atrocious, but I rejected it—just as I rejected the logic of my situation. I knew that even if I reached the shore, I was a mile from my truck. Even if I reached the truck, I was three miles from the road. And even if I reached the road, where was I? Alone.

I was still a hundred feet from the shore when the crocodiles caught up with me. I'd swum in crocodile-ridden waters before, so I knew what I had to do. Quickly, I changed the angle of my body, assuming an almost vertical position. My awkward crawl-stroke turned into a clumsy dog paddle. That made it difficult for the reptiles to seize me; their anatomy prevents them from turning their heads to the side.

Now I moved toward the shore much more slowly, splashing as violently as I could. One crocodile then shot forward like a green torpedo, and an instant later I heard a hollow clack at my ear—his jaws snapping shut.

Then, unbelievably, my feet touched the bottom, and I staggered out of the water, leaving behind me a fan-shaped flotilla of frustrated crocodiles.

My knees buckled and I sat down hard, right in the midst of the empty baskets my crew had abandoned. The stump of my wrist was still trickling blood, despite the pressure position. I knew that I'd somehow have to make a tourniquet in order to stop it.

Using my injured left hand and my teeth, I took one of my socks and managed to tie it around the upper part of my right arm. It was quite ineffective. I took the other one and knotted just above my elbow. The result was only a little better. Then I picked up a piece of liana vine from the ground and wound it tightly around my arm. The bleeding stopped—until the liana broke. I tried again, and the second one broke.

Finally, only a few feet away, half hidden by the creeping vines, I spotted a short length of rope lying on the ground, a fragment of an old fishing net. I slipped it over my arm and tightened it. Then I took one of the socks, wadded it into a hard ball, and stuffed it beneath the rope where it would press against the brachial artery. As a final touch, I wedged a small stick under the rope, and that slowed the bleeding to a negligible ooze.

That taken care of, I surveyed the other damage. There was no way of telling how badly my right eye was injured, but the entire right side of my face was one huge burned laceration. Those wounds had already clotted. My jaw and neck were both badly torn. A big flap of skin hung down on my collarbone, and the blood seeped down my chest. I pushed the skin back into place and it partially adhered.

The worst damage, aside from my missing right hand, was the condition of my left. Only the pinkie and the ring finger were intact. I might lose the first three fingers, perhaps the entire hand.

What sort of future lay ahead of me—if I survived? No hands, one eye, nearly deaf, and a scarred face. It was an appalling vision, but still I wanted to live—to feel things, do things and make things, whatever the difficulty.

The fact that I was alive at all was more than could have been expected. Only the complete instability of my position—standing up in a shaky canoe—saved me, because even dynamite has to work against some resistance.

I struggled to my feet, swayed and nearly fell to the ground, feeling an unbelievable pain and weakness in every part of my body. I took a step, then another and another through the green tunnel of bush. On and on, a hundred, five hundred, a thousand, two thousand painful steps—and then, with a feeling almost of disbelief, I saw a small patch of blue up ahead: the fender of my truck.

I climbed into the cab, slowly and awkwardly, and sat, immensely relieved to be off my feet. Now I felt that the worst physical exertion was behind me. I was filled with new confidence. Then I caught sight of myself in the rear view mirror.

A strange and terrible face stared back, but I examined it more with curiosity than emotion. The entire right side was encrusted with coagulated blood, and the skin was pocked everywhere with peculiar little holes. These, I learned later, contained splinters of bone, the fragments of my pulverized right hand.

The right eye was swollen shut, but at least it appeared to be intact. Both eyebrows were scored with long cuts, which I had inflicted with the naked bones of my arm.

I waited for a wave of nausea to pass, then, feeling a little better, started out on the three-mile journey to the road—in reverse.

I reached around the wheel to pull the gearshift lever into position with my two working fingers. Then, as I started to move backwards, I turned my head to the left to check my direction. But the tortured skin of my throat tore loose, and I had to stop to tuck it into position. A moment later, I was traveling backwards, trying to hold my head rigid as I watched the rearview mirror with my left eye.

Three miles in reverse on a dark jungle trail, snaking my way around tree trunks . . . and then blue sky and brilliant sunshine, back at the dusty road.

I paused a moment to relieve the tourniquet pressure, then shifted into second, then into third, shoving the lever down with my right elbow. The needle reached 50. I was finally on my way—but where?

During the 12 miles between the cove and the trading center of Nyanza-Lac, I had to find the answer. My ultimate destination, I knew, had to be the *Hôpital Rodhain* in Usumbura, at the northern tip of Lake Tanganyika. It was the only place where I could find qualified medical aid, the skill both to keep me alive and to save as much of my body as possible.

But Usumbura lay at the end of a road that wound 200 miles around more sharp curves and dangerous escarpments than any other of comparable length in all of Central Africa. It started at an altitude of 2,534 feet near Lake Tanganyika, then undulated wildly until it rose to 7,240 feet at Majejuru, then spiraled down dizzily toward the city nearly 5,000 feet below.

There was a serious complication at the summit of

Majejuru. After this point the road became so narrow that two cars couldn't pass simultaneously. So the next 18 miles was a "one-way road," sectioned off by a system of barriers. Cars traveling to the west during the evening hours had to reach Majejuru by nine o'clock. At that time, punctually, the barrier was closed and no traffic could pass toward Usumbura until 8:30 the next morning.

The time limit made it a gamble. But the odds were in my favor. Yet, as I forced myself to realize, that serpentine road through 200 miles of mountains was difficult enough for a normal man. It was obviously impossible for me. I knew that I would have to find help.

I considered the possibilities. The nearest place where I could count on finding competent aid was the Catholic Mission of the White Fathers at Makamba, 36 miles to the east.

It was a wild, crazy and thoroughly hair-raising drive. I steered around spectacular curves with two fingers, elbows and forearms, trying to make the maximum speed without going over the side. It was extremely painful, holding and turning the wheel through sudden changes of direction—but I made it.

I turned off into a long driveway that led to a cluster of imposing red brick buildings. Here among the White Fathers, I was sure to find someone to take me to Usumbura, to complete successfully the long, arduous drive.

I pulled to a stop, got out, and was shocked by my terrible weakness. I leaned against the hood, gasping a little as I tried to overcome the vertigo that threatened to sweep me under. Then a boy came running up, a sturdy little Muhutu native. He stopped short, petrified with fear at the unexpected vision confronting him: a towering white man, nearly naked, atrociously mutilated, and crusted from head to foot with coagulated blood.

"*Padri iko wapi?*" I asked—"Where is the Father?"

He swallowed several times. He licked his lips nervously and managed to stammer an answer. "*Padri Robert peke yake. Padri ingine yote iko ku safari,*" the boy said—"Father Robert is here alone. The others are all on safari." Then he backed away slowly until he collided with the wall.

I walked over to the massive wooden door of the refectory and banged on it with the side of my foot. A moment passed, and a white-robed priest opened the door, a slender man whom I had never seen here before. He stared at me with horror; his eyes widened and his face turned as white as his robe. He tried to speak, but the words never passed his lips. Instead, he buckled and slid toward the ground. Instinctively, I reached out to catch him with my right hand . . . and took most of his weight on the stump of my right wrist. The pain was unbelievable. I fought it for a long moment while I nearly bit through my lower lip. Then I poked at the fallen priest and called his name. Again, there was no answer.

"Isn't there anyone else here?" I asked the trembling native.

"*Hapana! Hapana!*"—"No!"

I tried again to revive Father Robert. Then I realized how I was wasting my precious time. Even if he managed to compose himself enough to start out with me, he was obviously nervous and undependable—and probably a bad driver.

I walked back to my truck. Each step took enormous, sickening effort, but once again I felt relief the moment I sat down. I loosened the tourniquet, then drove away toward the northwest.

Now that Makamba had failed me, I had to try to reach Bururi, my own territorial post about 40 miles away. This stretch of road was relatively easy, but I felt much weaker since the incident at the mission, and the pain was more difficult to endure.

About 45 minutes later I pulled into Bururi, just as the last remnants of the sunset were fading. I felt relieved when I saw the familiar little government headquarters and the night watchman dozing on the front steps.

I called out and he woke with a start. Then his eyes became almost circular with recognition, astonishment, shock and fear. A moment later, after an exchange of Swahili questions and answers, I found out that Bururi was just as hopeless as Makamba: the three men I had counted on were away. The only European in the area was a rookie, newly arrived from Belgium.

I knocked on his door with my foot. After a moment it opened, and I thought at first that he was about to follow Father Robert's example. He stared, whitened, and seemed ready to faint.

He did volunteer to take me to Usumbura, though,

but to his astonishment I turned him down. A short conversation had confirmed my instinctive decision, especially the fact that he had only recently learned how to drive. I thought of a nervous, newly hatched driver piddling along cautiously toward the nine o'clock barrier and finding it closed.

When I started off again, it was a little past seven o'clock. Four hours had passed since the explosion, and I had less than two hours left to travel some 80 miles to the barrier. Several times on the road I felt myself starting to fall into a stupor, but I fought to stay awake by singing. Soon I was inconceivably thirsty; my whole body seemed to cry out for water with profound physiological urgency.

After an interminable period of the thirst, the cold, and the never-ending pain, I saw ahead, with a sense of shock, that I was coming to a marker only ten miles from the barrier.

What time was it now? I had no way of knowing, but it must have been well past 8:30. Perhaps it was already nine. I pushed the throttle down to the floor, and the truck shot ahead at 60, a dangerous speed for this type of road. The landscape rushed backward in a green haze of banana plantations, and in less than five minutes I saw an important fork loom up ahead.

I slowed and started to swing into the left turn. Then, at the last moment, I became aware of a truck on my blind right side. I swung the wheel to the left, missing it by inches, then skidded crazily, and hung onto the wheel with my two sound fingers, fighting to keep control. I rocketed off the road, skimmed past a huge Grevillea tree, ricocheted to the opposite shoulder, and finally bounced back onto the road. Miraculously, I was still pointed in the right direction.

My fingers were bleeding badly, and I was shaken by the close call. But I speeded up again, feeling a strange mixture of relief and anxiety. The fact that the truck was traveling at that speed meant only one thing: the driver was trying to make the barrier at Majejuru before it closed. It wasn't nine o'clock yet, and I still had a chance to live.

I caught up with him, hovering at his tail in the cloud of dust from his wheels. I started to pass and then fell back; the road at this point was a series of blind curves. I sounded my horn again and again, but he refused to pull over. He had slowed me down at least 15, perhaps 30 miles an hour. That could cost up to five minutes in the race, five minutes that could save my life.

I swung out to the left with my gas pedal down to the floor. But the curve was sharper than I thought; the pickup skidded and nearly went off on the shoulder again. I clawed at the wheel with my bleeding hand and swung back to the right—almost too far. Then the truck was behind me.

Those last ten miles to the barrier could never have been measured with a clock. I drove through an endless hour of motion that must have lasted only eight or nine minutes. For the first time since the blast, I was able to forget the pain. All of my conscious thought was fixed on one frightful vision: a native guard placing a heavy padlock on a red-and-white striped wooden arm that stretched across the road. The lock clicked shut, and he mounted his motor cycle to start on the scheduled inspection of the 18-mile strip.

I covered the remaining distance in an agony of doubt. Then I swung around the last curve and saw the guard coming down from his hut on the hill, his motorcycle waiting on the shoulder, and the red-and-white arm of the barrier. It was still pointing to heaven. I drove past it, stopped about 30 feet beyond, loosened the tourniquet, and watched as the native reached the bottom of the hill. The striped wooden arm fell and the padlock clicked into place behind me—and in front of the truck.

But I hadn't made it yet. Usumbura lay ahead, across 30 miles that spiraled 5,000 feet down toward the lake in great looping jug handles.

The first 18-mile stretch was the narrow, precipitous and thoroughly notorious "one-way road." Many people, including good drivers, were reluctant to cover those miles, even after years in Urundi.

But I wasn't. With two fingers, with elbows and forearms, I hung onto the wheel, peering through the gathering mist with one eye dazed with pain. The mist deepened—or was it the pain?—and then I felt myself slipping away, into a beautiful, easy oblivion. "I am awake!" I shouted. "I *am* awake! And I won't close my eyes!"

I drove on slowly, fighting my way around mile

after mile of curves. Then, gradually, I became aware of a new sensation: I had to urinate. Oddly enough, this single urge strengthened my confidence. It demonstrated that, despite all the blood I had lost, urine was still filtering through my kidneys. That proved my blood pressure was still above the critical level beneath which no urine could be produced. The obvious answer to my new problem was to follow my impulse without stopping the truck. But that idea outraged my dignity.

I pulled to a stop and eased out of the cab. Then I took two steps toward the edge of the escarpment, paused, surveyed the tremendous gulf, then with a gesture which I considered supremely defiant, I made an impressive trajectory that fell over the cliff for at least 2,000 feet. Then I staggered back into the truck.

The last 12 miles were an unbroken succession of smooth curves. The road itself was far less dangerous now, but the mist was thicker and I had to watch for opposing traffic. After four or five miles the mist cleared and I caught my first glimpse of Usumbura, a shower of golden lights next to the moonlit waves of Lake Tanganyika. It seemed like an impossibly beautiful vision. Then I saw another vision: a gas gauge that registered empty. I was outraged. It would have been too stupid, too meaningless to lose everything now. I kept my eyes fixed on the road and the glorious lights of Usumbura, trying to ignore the ominous needle that pointed without wavering to "E."

I drove on, conscious of every tenth of a mile. Then

I saw the metal bridge that crosses the Muha River at the southern edge of the town. The pickup and I rattled across. I was indeed at the limit of my long ordeal, and, perhaps, my life.

I drove a mile and stopped at the entrance of the *Hôpital Rodhain*, and struggled to get out of the cab. I swayed and caught the handle of the door with my two good fingers, trembling, trying not to buckle and fall.

The *Infirmier de Service*—a tall native in a white shirt—saw me standing next to the truck, clutching at the door. His jaw dropped and he started to run toward me. Then he rushed back into the hospital, shouting for the doctors and nurse.

Three weeks later, I was back at the wheel of my pickup, driving south to the cove for a little showdown with my six Bagoma fishermen. My right hand was, of course, gone, and I'd lost 75 percent of my hearing. But I'd kept both of my eyes—although my vision would never be perfect again—and I still had five fingers on my bandaged left hand.

Death and the Friendly River

BY SCOTT SEEGERS

5

This is one of those adventures that just happen, unforewarned. You do something that is safe; you know it is because you've tried it a dozen times before. But then something goes wrong, and a commonplace event becomes a catastrophe.

• For several winters my wife Katie and I had promised ourselves that the next time there was a really good snow on the ground we would row out to the big rock near the far side of the Potomac River and take some pictures of our house. The site is spectacular. The heavily forested Virginia shore at that point rises almost as steeply as a cliff, and our house is perched on a hilltop high above. From the rock, the turbulence of Yellow Falls just downstream would make a dramatic foreground; by combining it with the snow-covered hillside reaching up to the house, we hoped to produce a stunning photograph.

Last February, a foot of new snow glistened under brilliant sunlight. It was bitter cold, but achingly beautiful. "We'll never have a better day for it," I said. "Let's go."

We were on good terms with this stretch of the Potomac, located a few miles above Washington. It was a member of the family, the place our kids had learned to swim and on whose sun-drenched rocks we had picnicked for years. But this amiable river, *our* river, would teach us that day a lesson we will never forget.

The roundabout track down to the river had once been a wagon road leading to a small gold mine, now long abandoned. Although decades of spring rains have dotted it with deep holes, our jeep would take us to the river's edge and back, except that in two places on the return trip I would have to hook a cable to a tree and use our power winch to drag us over obstructions.

Through the woods and down the steep hill we went, our eight-foot aluminum skiff sliding behind us as gaily as a sleigh. At the shore, I carefully loaded my cameras into the skiff. Bundled into layers of heavy clothes, booted and gloved, we clumsily got aboard and shoved off.

The river was high and the current swift, but I launched the skiff well upstream of the big rock. It was no problem to row across, then drift down upon the rock. As we swept past, I grabbed a little scrub maple and pulled us ashore. I had done it many times before.

I tied up the skiff, brushed the snow from the rock,

and carefully climbed to its top. The view of the house *was* magnificent. In the foreground, the falls leaped like molten sapphires in the intense sunlight. One at a time, Katie handed up the cameras, some with normal, others with telephoto lenses. To be sure of getting just the photos I wanted, I took several shots with each.

Carefully, Katie stowed the cameras and sat down in the stern of the skiff. I climbed aboard and set the oars in the oarlocks. But, still bemused by the beauty of the scene, I pushed away from the rock while still standing, instead of sitting down and being ready to row the moment I cast off. Before I could sit down, the current had caught the skiff and whirled it past the rock. The falls were not more than 40 feet away.

I dropped to the seat and pulled as powerfully as I could on the oars. The skiff hesitated an instant as the blades bit into the water. We would have escaped the pull of the falls if one oar had not hit a barely submerged rock and jumped from the oarlock. The lopsided thrust threw the boat crosswise to the current, and we raced toward the falls.

At this particular spot, the falls are in three steps, the last and largest a drop of about two feet into a deep, swirling pool. The skiff bounced gently as it went sidewise over the first step. I got the oar back in the oarlock and straightened the boat out as we dropped over the second step in a welter of foam. There was no chance of getting upstream now, but no water had yet come aboard. I had an instant's wild hope that we might also live through the last drop. "Hold tight," I said to Katie. "Here we go." The skiff bucked like a wild stallion—and the world exploded.

I came to the surface clutching at the overturned skiff. Katie was beside me, also holding on. The paralyzing cold squeezed my chest with steel bands. I could hardly breathe. In a voice that sounded like a rundown Victrola, I said, "Hang onto the boat. Kick and paddle toward shore."

We were in the main branch of the river, about 250 feet from the Virginia shore and our waiting jeep. Although we kicked and paddled mightily, our booted legs and gloved hands were heavy and nearly useless, and the current carried us rapidly downstream. I spared a few seconds to watch the fine black leather case containing my new Graflex disappear in the water.

Suddenly, with a crash, the current brought the skiff up against a large boulder. As if in slow motion, we struggled onto the rock and took stock. The oars were gone. Although I managed somehow to turn the boat over, it remained half under water, riveted against the rock by the current. I tugged at the skiff for almost ten minutes, but I could not drag it high enough up the rock to bail. "We'll have to leave the boat," I said.

We took off our boots and heavy outer clothing. With fingers as numb as sticks, I removed the skiff's mooring line and tied one end to Katie's wrist. Holding onto the other end, I started wading out on a submerged bar. "I'm going to try to get to that rock," I

told her, pointing to a boulder a little way out in the racing channel between us and shore. "If the rope reaches, I'll pull you over. If it isn't long enough, jump in the instant it tightens."

The savage cold hurt like an enormous toothache. (The water temperature was 35 degrees, the air temperature 20, we learned later.) But we were not frightened, simply because we had not realized how desperate our plight was. We couldn't swim in our remaining clothes, but we knew that by keeping our feet down when we went under we would soon hit a shallow or a rock on which to push to the surface for another breath. And if we consistently pushed toward shore, we would make it. Then it would be only a matter of walking back through the forest to the jeep, getting home, and building a fire. Or so we thought.

I launched myself into deep water and plummeted to the bottom. The current whirled me along, banging my legs against underwater rocks. Finally, I got my feet under me, kicked hard against the bottom, and sailed toward daylight. Too soon, I opened my mouth to breathe—and got instead a big swallow of Potomac. I felt surprised and indignant. "Our" river was trying to drown me! The next time up I got air instead of water, and then I sank again.

I missed the rock I was aiming for, but fetched up on another one downstream. Katie had hit the water the instant the rope tightened, and a moment later she was beside me. I don't know how many similar rock-to-rock traverses we made, but we finally stumbled ashore about 400 yards downstream from the jeep. "The worst is over," I said to Katie. I was wrong.

The shore rose above us in a steep bank some eight feet high. Even on her hands and knees, Katie could not make the climb. Hanging onto each other, we floundered along through the ice and tangled roots at the water's edge until the bank leveled off. Katie fell frequently, and each time she fell she pulled me down with her. Within a few minutes I no longer had the strength to pull her to her feet.

We began progressing by trees. We would stumble a few steps, then fall. I would scramble to my feet and try to pull Katie along until we reached a tree. Using the tree as a prop, we would get her upright and aimed for another tree. Then the next tree, one at a time.

With the soft gray fuzz of oblivion lapping at the edges of our consciousness, we tottered and crawled through a little clearing from which we could look up at our home. It sat less than 500 feet away, straight up the hill. But it might as well have been on the moon for any chance we had of climbing the precipitous slope.

About 150 yards from the jeep, Katie fell for the last time. "I can't go any farther," she mumbled, lying face down in the snow. I shook her. "You've got to keep moving," I said. She did not respond.

"I'll go get the jeep and come back for you," I said. She never heard me. I staggered toward the jeep. Suddenly the trees went into a wild dance, and the ground rose and hit me in the face. I fell every time my numb feet hit a stone. With maybe 75 yards to go, I could not get up again. I crawled to the nearest tree, pulled and shoved myself upright. Through lips too stiff to form the words properly, a voice groaned, "I'll be damned if I'll freeze to death this close."

I shoved myself away from the tree, staggered a dozen steps, fell, and crawled to the next tree. I no longer felt cold. There was room in my mind for only one thought. *Jeep.* The world was a red jeep.

Suddenly I was there, groping at the door, dragging myself into the seat. Concentrating like a chess master, I looked at the instrument panel. The ignition lock swam into focus. I fumbled the key into it. *Choke.* With a cold motor the jeep will not start unless choked. My useless fingers slipped off the choke button. I used both hands, and both slipped off. The choke was the center of the universe. *Pull the choke out.* A partly opened wrench lay on the floor. I slid the jaws over the choke shaft, got my hands behind the wrench and pulled. The choke came out. I could not turn the ignition key. I used the wrench again. The motor sputtered into life.

I pawed at the steering wheel for a precious minute before realizing that my hands would not grip it. I hooked my wrists over the spokes, then cautiously piloted the jeep across the rocks to where Katie lay. I do not remember rousing her and cannot imagine how she got into the jeep. With the glimmer of consciousness left to me, I gave myself step-by-step instructions.

I must remember not to turn around here because the trees are too close. Back up. I poked a few times at the gear shift, and it finally slid into reverse. The jeep backed erratically to a more open spot. I turned it around and put the accelerator to the floor. Weaving crazily, the forest fled past on both sides. *I must not try the gold-mine road we came down because I cannot handle the winch and cable. Try the track up the other side of the valley.* Roaring wide open in four-wheel drive, the jeep plowed along the twisting track up the ridge. It came out on top at the home of a neighbor. He must have seen the jeep coming because he opened his door instantly. Faces floated before me. They got Katie out of the jeep.

My memories of the rest are confused. Someone gave me brandy. Someone else dabbed at my face with a cloth, and I realized that saliva was streaming out of both corners of my mouth. I was lying on the floor before a big fire, shaking uncontrollably and making strange involuntary noises. Through the fog came Katie's voice: "Darling, are you all right?"

"No," I mumbled ungraciously, "I'm cold."

I passed out then, and was roused by a squirt of oxygen administered by the local Rescue Squad. They took us to the hospital, packed a score of gorgeous hot-water bags around each of us, and gave us typhoid and tetanus shots. From the waist down, our bodies were a mosaic of bruises and cuts from being banged against the rocks, but nothing was broken.

They took our temperatures. Katie's was 92 degrees. This was about two hours after we arrived at the neighbor's house. I learned later that cold-weather-survival specialists consider 88 degrees the lowest body temperature from which one normally can be expected to recover. Katie must have been very close to the edge.

We still love the river. But we will never again think of it as one of the family. It is a body of moving water, beautiful in its still pools, in its swift-running channels, and where it foams over the rocks below the house. But it is without conscience. If you forget that it obeys only the law of gravity, it can quite casually kill you.

Doomsday Mountain

BY NICHOLAS B. CLINCH

6

In the northwest corner of Pakistan, high in the Himalayas, looms a 25,660-foot giant called Masherbrum—"Doomsday Mountain." Three times in the past, well-equipped, hard-driving mountaineers have tried to climb it. Two of them died on its slopes, dozens of others were injured, and none reached the top.

Then in 1960 a team of Americans and Pakistanis tried once again.

• Sound is deceptive, often elusive, high in the Himalaya. I was in a tent at 23,000 feet with a Pakistani mountain climber, Captain Jawed Akhter, when an alien sound made us look at each other in alarm. Was it a call for help or just a variation in the whine of the wind and the hum of our cooking stove? We couldn't tell. We were stormbound high up on the side of Masherbrum. Above us, four climbers were waiting for the storm to end so they could make a try for the summit.

Then we heard the sound again—an unmistakable yell for help from above. Jamming on our boots, Akhter and I scrambled out of our tent just in time to see, through the parting mist and snow, three figures struggling to keep their feet in the wake of a small avalanche. Where was the fourth man? Who was missing?

But before I tell how our luck nearly ran out on Masherbrum, I'd better explain how we happened to be there in the first place. The idea of climbing the mountain was put in my mind two years ago at the completion of another Himalayan climb. We were stumbling wearily down the Baltoro Glacier after having made the first ascent of Hidden Peak when one of our group pointed enthusiastically to a tremendous tower of rock and ice to the south. "Come on back and let's try Masherbrum," he said. The rest of us just shook our heads. The last thing we were interested in at that moment was another Himalayan peak.

But if you are a climber, you soon tend to forget about the difficulties of financing a Himalayan expedition, the headaches of organization and even the special agonies of high-altitude climbing, when the combination of blazing sun and snow makes you feel as if your head were in an oven and your feet in a freezer. Instead, you remember the comradeship of men who face a common hazard, the exhilaration of success and, above all, the magnificent mountains.

So after we were back home, I talked with George Bell—a nuclear physicist from Los Alamos, New Mexico, and an experienced climber—about another Himalayan climb, and we looked for others who wanted to tackle Masherbrum. Eventually we formed a ten-man party under Bell's leadership.

From Seattle, Washington, came Dick McGowan, a young geography teacher who was the chief guide on Mount Rainier during the summer. Dick had been on three Alaskan expeditions, among others.

Dr. Tom Hornbein from St. Louis, Missouri, was our triple-threat man—mountaineer, physician and high-altitude physiologist. One of the original members of the Rocky Mountain Rescue Group, he has done many extremely difficult ascents throughout the United States.

Willi Unsoeld, assistant professor of philosophy and comparative religion at Oregon State College, and Dick Emerson, assistant professor of sociology at the University of Cincinnati, both experienced mountaineers, rounded out the expedition's "faculty."

Our three Pakistani mountaineers—Akhter, Imtiaz Azim and Mohd Akram Qureshi—were captains in the Pakistan Army and were well schooled in the peculiar problems of the Himalayas.

Tom McCormack, a twenty-five-year-old ranger from Rio Vista, California, and I, a twenty-nine-year-old attorney from Dallas, Texas, completed the team. We had climbed together before in a few places, including Hidden Peak.

It is a mountaineering saying that each expedition stands on the shoulders of its predecessors. This was especially true with us. Major James Waller and Joe

Walmsley, leaders of previous expeditions that tried to climb Masherbrum, gave us complete information on the obstacles that had to be overcome. In 1938 Waller had led a British party that reached 24,000 feet before storms and avalanches drove them back. Two of the climbers were badly frostbitten and lost all their toes and parts of their fingers.

A New Zealand party made the next attempt in April 1955. The men were plagued by deep snow, and one of them died of pneumonia. They turned back, too.

Then in 1957 the British returned, led by Walmsley. For nine weeks they struggled. One climber died of pneumonia, but they refused to quit. Two of them, Walmsley and Don Whillans, climbed to within 300 feet of the summit before being driven back by the difficulties of the rock and the oncoming darkness.

We felt we had a reasonable chance to crack that last unclimbed 300 feet. Masherbrum has twin summits; the one on the east is the higher by fifty feet. A snow *couloir*—a narrow gully—runs up between these peaks and gives access to the final ridge. If we could only climb that gully—but in 1957 the British had found the snow too treacherous and were forced to try the adjoining rocks.

Thus we prepared ourselves for the worst. By mid-March 1960, we had gathered four and a half tons of supplies and had them shipped to Pakistan. Then on May 18, we assembled with our equipment in Rawalpindi after a 950-mile train ride from Karachi. Heavily laden DC-3's carried us through the Himalaya to Skardu, where we spent several days repacking our gear into sixty-pound loads. There we met our six high-altitude porters, whom we called HAP's.

Next came a long hike to the mountain's base. Eighteen miles to Gol, 22 to Gwari—sun, sand and blisters. Some of us began to think we would never live to see the mountain. Finally we began the last leg of our march, 30 miles up the narrow Hushe valley. Granite spires rose above the dark green, irrigated fields that punctuated the sandy waste. For two days we followed the trail along the Hushe River, crossing and recrossing rickety log bridges before reaching the last village.

Then we started up the rock-covered moraine of the Masherbrum glacier. It was a 12-mile hike, a long, hard day. The upper part of the glacier was still covered by the winter's snows, but at 5:00 P.M. on May 30, our expedition reached its base campsite, 13,500 feet high.

We spent the next day getting our equipment reorganized for the climb. Some of the thirty oxygen bottles we had brought were low in pressure, and half of the valves leaked when we turned them on. It was disappointing, but we were able to muster up around a dozen good bottles—enough for a couple of summit assaults.

That evening we gathered in our big white tent for a council of war. We knew where we had to go. First we had to wend our way among the tall ice pinnacles, watching carefully for crevasses, as we crossed the

Serac Glacier to a snow basin that nestled beneath hanging ice cliffs. From there the route went up steep slopes that culminated in a dome. From the dome we would go to a plateau under the final southeast face.

We decided that Camp One should be pitched at about 15,500 feet on the glacier. Camp Two would be established somewhere in the basin. Our advance base for the upper part of the mountain would be Camp Three, at 21,000 feet, on top of the dome. Despite the information we had from our predecessors, we would still have to locate and prepare the trail, as well as determine the safest sites for the camps. While this reconnaissance was going on, the rest of the expedition would carry loads of supplies up the mountain.

There was now an unprecedented spell of good weather. On June 1, McGowan, Emerson, Hornbein and Akhter found the way to Camp One. The key was an avalanche chute on the right side of the glacier which the British had named Scaly Alley because of the numerous falling rocks. A bit nervous, we climbed early in the morning when there was less danger of avalanches. There were no accidents, and our morale improved. Furthermore, deep snow covered the crevasses. This made it possible for porters, who had no special climbing equipment, to make the ascent, provided they were escorted along safe routes.

We put McGowan in charge of this exercise in mass mountaineering on the theory that his experience in dragging tourists up Mount Rainier left him uniquely qualified for the task. Five days later we had carried

3,000 pounds of supplies up to Camp One and had largely abandoned base camp.

Meanwhile, Unsoeld and McCormack located Camp Two at 19,500 feet on the slopes leading to the dome. No one liked the place because of the potential danger from snow slides, but there wasn't much choice. In 1955 the New Zealanders' food dump down in the basin had been buried by a gigantic ice avalanche. We avoided staying in that camp as much as possible.

On June 8, McGowan, Akhter and Unsoeld, starting from Camp Two, climbed to the top of the dome, putting in fixed ropes as they went. The HAP's brought up load after load of food and equipment, and Camp Three was established.

Then the weather changed. It snowed every day for 24 days, but we were able to keep moving, and with a great effort, Bell, Emerson and McCormack pioneered the way to Camp Four at 22,000 feet. Then McGowan and Unsoeld put in Camp Five at the base of the southeast face, and the endless job of relaying supplies continued. Every night the snow covered our tracks; every day we rebroke the trail. Bamboo wands topped with triangular flags were stuck into the snow every 100 feet to mark the route. On some days the snow and fog were so bad we could see only two wands ahead.

Behind us the soft snow on the Serac Glacier was melting, and crevasses were opening up. Once when Captain Qureshi and I took five porters along a much-traveled route down to Base Camp, a weakened snow bridge collapsed, and I sank chin-deep in a crevasse. Ahead of us the southeast face swept 3,000 feet upward at an average angle of forty-five degrees to the twin peaks. On it were many overhanging ice cliffs; the largest was more than 200 feet high. If that cliff broke off, it would annihilate anything in its path.

Camp Five was the dividing line. Below it we felt we would have been unlucky to get killed; above it we would be lucky to escape. We lived in a tilted world of wind, snow and avalanches that rumbled past after every storm. Base Camp seemed as remote as New York City.

We pushed on. A good day was due soon, and we wanted to be in position. Unsoeld and McGowan, the first assault team, led up and across the face. I followed, escorting five HAP's. We were under the gun of the large ice cliff and could not find a safe place for Camp Six. Finally Unsoeld spotted a sheltered area behind a 30-foot ice pinnacle that would hold two tents. The next day Bell and Hornbein joined us.

On June 24, Unsoeld and McGowan started for the summit, each carrying two bottles of oxygen. But they ran into trouble with their gear and had to abandon the bottles. The climbing became more difficult then; in many places the snow lay just a few inches over the ice. One particular traverse above the ice cliffs was especially delicate. The fragile steps they were kicking in the snow were in danger of collapsing, and they could get only a "psychological belay," a weak stance that wouldn't hold a fall.

At noon, when they had climbed to 25,000 feet, Unsoeld and McGowan reached a bergschrund—a big crevasse formed at the head of a glacier by the moving ice pulling away from the mountain. It cut across the snow face underneath the twin summits. But then the weather turned bad again, and they decided another camp was needed before they could try for the top. They left a cache of *pitons* and descended through the storm. Small slides of powder snow started coming down.

Suddenly, McGowan was swept from his steps. Fortunately, Unsoeld had a good stance and was able to hold him. But it was a warning of things to come.

The first attempt had failed, but at least they knew what they were up against, and the route was prepared to Camp Seven. The four men waited for a break in the weather. It never came. When they looked from their tents on the morning of June 27 and saw a new storm bearing down on them, they decided to retreat. Descending cautiously through a wicked mixture of snow and mist, they followed the bamboo wands.

They were slowly groping their way forward when the avalanche hit. First the powder snow was around their ankles; a split second later it was over their heads. Desperately they tried to drive in their axes, but one by one they were swept downhill, first Hornbein, then Bell, then McGowan. Unsoeld, now the highest man, almost held; then he, too, was flipped backward.

But he came right side up again as the avalanche was slowing down. He redrove his ax, and this time it held. The four men had slid 200 feet, and had come to a stop just short of an ice cliff.

Their shouts after they got free of the deep snow were the ones Akhter and I heard in our tent. McGowan was the climber I couldn't see when I started struggling uphill. His arms had been pinned by the climbing rope, and he had been dragged down the hill under the snow. But he dug himself out, and after resting a few moments, was able to stumble into camp unaided.

We regrouped. Hornbein and McGowan went to Camp Three to recuperate, while the rest of us occupied the two tents, waiting for any change in the weather. Snow and wind, wind and snow—avalanches constantly thundered down the face. The supplies which had seemed so enormous four weeks before began to shrink.

On July 4 the weather cleared, and next morning Bell, Unsoeld, Emerson and Akhter climbed up to the bergschrund. The cache containing our rock *pitons* had been swept away. There was very little space for a tent, but they managed to pitch one at an angle, partly on the lip of the bergschrund itself, partly on the snow inside the crevasse. Akhter descended, and the others settled in. During the night ice pellets struck the side of the tent. For a few bad moments the occupants thought an avalanche was coming and they were going to be

pushed over the edge. They shifted themselves toward the back of the tent, and nobody slept that night.

Five o'clock next morning they left camp and followed the bergschrund laterally until they were directly below the steep *couloir* that led to the summit ridge. The weather was perfect—too perfect; the sun beat upon them unmercifully. Stifling in the heat, they climbed upward. Cautiously picking their way across a band of rock, they entered the gully. On the right the ice was exposed; on the left it was covered with treacherous fluffy snow. Between the ice and the fluff they kicked a fragile ladder of steps.

Six hours later they reached the razor-sharp ridge between the twin peaks and turned toward the East Peak. But they were blocked on the ridge by a gendarme, a large rock tower. Unsoeld hammered an ice screw into a crack of the rock, clipped a rope in for protection and inched his way over loose, snow-covered rocks. Again they balanced along the thin snow edge until they reached a vertical rock wall 40 feet high. A short smooth chimney—a crack wide enough to enable a person to get inside—was the only possible route. In the Rockies it would have been a minor problem; at 25,500 feet it was absolutely exhausting. Unsoeld and Bell heaved themselves upward. Now there was only a gentle slope ahead. Rhythmically, mechanically, they plodded through the soft snow. Then the ridge slanted downward.

It was 3:15 in the afternoon. They were on top!

The giants of the upper Baltoro Glacier rose before

them: Hidden Peak, Gasherbrum IV, Broad Peak and, above all, K2, second highest mountain in the world. The two men took photographs for an hour, then started down, attaching their ropes to four-foot aluminum pickets and rappelling down the 50-degree slope of the gulley. They got back to their tent by 8:00 P.M. They weren't the only climbers who had an exciting afternoon. The second assault party, Akhter, Hornbein and McGowan, was starting up the fixed ropes toward Camp Seven when McGowan, who had never completely recovered from the avalanche, doubled over with violent cramps. Hornbein yelled, "We've got to go back!" Akhter, in the lead, turned around. His delicate snow step broke, and he came toppling down the slope. In desperation Hornbein grabbed the fixed rope with his left hand and the climbing rope with his right. If he didn't hold, all three climbers would go over the ice cliff below.

He held. Akhter tumbled down the slope and then plunged deep into the snow when the rope went taut. It was 160 feet from drop to stop. Akhter was all right, but McGowan was out of action now, so all returned to Camp Six.

The following day, July 7, Emerson, Akhter and I prepared to make the next attempt. Unsoeld and Bell had plenty of good advice, the essence of which was "Be careful."

After reaching the bergschrund, we tried to widen the snow platform and repitch the tent, but it still tilted downward and hung out over the slope. During the night Emerson began suffering from an attack of dysentery, but he wouldn't think of quitting.

We wanted to get an early start for the summit, so at 1:00 A.M. on July 8, Akhter and I lighted a stove and began melting snow for breakfast. That done, we punctured a can of butane to light a second stove. But the valve was defective and before we realized it the escaping stream of gas hit the flame of the first stove. Instantly a fountain of fire shot to the top of the tent, setting the inner lining ablaze. I threw the pot of melted snow on it, but it kept on burning.

We had to get out. Gingerly I went for the entrance of the tent farthest from the flames—we had to be careful or we'd knock ourselves off the mountain. I unzipped one of the two zippers—and the flap opened into space. I started to unzip the other. It jammed.

Emerson finally woke up to find his head surrounded by flames. He tried to get out, but I was in his way, so he stood fumbling for his knife to cut a hole in the side of the tent. Meanwhile, Akhter, his retreat blocked, picked up a pair of pants and beat out the fire.

After having nearly cooked ourselves for breakfast, we felt somewhat disorganized. Furthermore, Emerson was now too sick to go for the summit, but he insisted that Akhter and I make the attempt while he cleaned up the mess. The two of us left at 7:30.

I tried to use oxygen, but the rig was troublesome and eventually I gave it up. Akhter and I, rotating the lead, slowly climbed up the gully. The steps had filled with frozen snow; we had to rekick every one. We reached the ridge and headed east. I tiptoed across the gendarme while Jawed struggled up the chimney.

Then there were no more tracks to follow. We were on the summit of Masherbrum! But it was almost nightfall, and we had time only to take a few pictures before we had to start down again. And our troubles weren't over yet. As we rappelled down the vertical rock wall, one of Akhter's down overmitts became untied and disappeared into the closing darkness. The thin air was blurring our minds, and I foolishly clipped my ice ax to my belt to free my hands. As I started off an overhang on the rope, the ax twisted and jammed on a ledge, leaving me suspended in mid-air. I freed it only on the third frantic try.

What happened on the next rappel was even more critical. We were using two ropes tied together so we could slide 120 feet at a time. It was still dark, for the moon had not risen. Standing in the *couloir*, we pulled on the ropes. The first one came. The second one cleared the sling and started to drop, but suddenly it stuck. We put all our weight on it, but it refused to budge. We *had* to rappel because the gully was too dangerous to climb down; but now, with just one rope, we could not possibly reach the aluminum pickets put in by Unsoeld and Bell. We would have to cut a deep channel into the snow to use as an anchor for our remaining rope.

This doesn't sound very difficult, but at 25,300 feet in the bitter cold, it took ages. Hour after hour we worked, first in darkness, then in the welcome light of the moon. We spent the whole night cutting that channel, and finally reached our scorched tent at 7:30 in the morning, 24 hours after we had left it.

Both of us were exhausted, and Akhter's fingers and toes were frostbitten. (Later he lost the tip of one finger.) Time was precious now. Next day we packed Camp Seven and began the retreat. Emerson, Akhter and I stumbled down the lines to Camp Six.

The next day a storm broke. We knew we had only a few hours to get to Camp Five before the powder-snow avalanches started. We were desperately tired, stumbling, and our snow steps were collapsing under us. The situation was serious.

Then we saw two figures in the mist. Willi Unsoeld and Tom Hornbein had come up from Camp Five to inquire if we wanted assistance. We did. They took our packs and guided us down through the swirling snow. Measuring distances with the rope, they did a brilliant job of blind navigation.

An hour later, as we reached Camp Five, the newly fallen snow began to avalanche far up the mountain behind us. But now we didn't care.

"We Rowed . . . and Rowed . . . and Rowed"

BY JOHN FAIRFAX

7

In 1969 a Britisher named John Fairfax became the first person to row across the Atlantic Ocean—alone. This 4,000-mile feat left only one major challenge for the oarsman: the Pacific Ocean, the largest body of water on earth.

But he needed a partner. He selected Sylvia Cook, a woman friend who had ten years' experience on a rowing team. In their 35-foot rowboat of mahogany specially designed for the journey, they experienced weeks of gale winds, skin burned raw by sun and drenched by water, endless drudgery and exhausting labor—and several near-fatal mishaps. The trip took an entire year.

John and Sylvia had trained for nearly a year before—rowing, running, dieting to add weight that later could be lost—and on April 26, 1971, they shoved off from a San Francisco dock. But bad weather and a broken transceiver forced them to round back for repairs. After three weeks in Ensenada, Mexico, they started out again . . .

- Out of Ensenada at last, Sylvia and I tried to put in 15 hours of rowing a day. I would row ten, she five. At times, though, the sea was too choppy for rowing, so we allowed the boat to drift, keeping a course by playing the winds and currents with our rudder. When we got too far off course, we'd pull with the oars until we were back in the general direction we wanted. It was a difficult task, made all the more difficult by the swarm of sand flies that joined us in Mexico and stayed with us for practically the whole year.

Britannia II was designed with low freeboard (the height of the hull above the water) to facilitate rowing, which it did. But it also kept us wet, constantly wet, even in flat seas. For 105 days, we rowed and we rowed *and* we rowed. Shark scares and the approach of an occasional whale were all that broke the seemingly endless routine.

Yet there was no leisure to speak of. When not rowing, we always had other chores to do, and the rowing would leave us in constant need of rest. I would row about two hours, pause for 15 minutes, then start again. When the temperature hit the high 90s we rowed mostly at night to avoid dehydration.

Our first landfall after leaving Ensenada was Washington Island. We put in on October 6 for the purpose of replenishing our water supply, which was dangerously low. Also, our transceiver had broken down, our sea anchors had rotted away, and our battery-charging generator had failed.

It was more than a month before we got going

again, and when we did, on November 12th, our Mexican sand flies came right along.

We were worried one of us might come down with Dengue fever (we never did), because it was erupting all over the Gilbert Islands at that time. But what weighted on us most in the next two months was the deadly day-to-day monotony. After our brief holiday in the paradise of Washington Island the ordeal of tedium seemed worse than ever. We rowed, Sylvia cooked and kept us generally shipshape, and we dueled with the wind.

We celebrated the Christmas season on the high seas. Our whole champagne supply went into it, and we got properly drunk for the occasion of crossing the international date line from January 1, 1972, to January 1, 1972.

It almost proved to be a *last* festival.

What happened was my own fault. We had sighted Onotoa, an outlying island of the Gilberts, at dawn on the ninth of January. According to my calculations we were about 17 miles east of it. We had had no luck with the transmitter since leaving Washington Island and hence were still without a two-way radio. Almost two months had passed without two-way communication. We wanted to get a message to our parents and sponsors, so we found Onotoa on our charts and made for it.

On approaching, we saw what looked like a gap dividing the island in two. There was no doubt it lacked the breadth for a sizable craft, but we thought ours was small enough to slip through, so we made for it, even though I knew it was on the weather side. To approach a coral atoll on the weather side in a rowboat, with a ten-knot wind behind, is lousy seamanship in any circumstances. To do so without a clue to the lay of the place is lunacy. But Onotoa is 12 miles long, and although it would have been easy enough to round the island while we were still ten miles off, it would have meant an extra ten or 20 miles of rowing. We hadn't slept in three days, which undoubtedly impaired my judgment. Instead of taking the safest course, I chose the shortest.

As we drew close to the low, flat atoll, we discovered to our horror that the passage was blocked by tiny islets and a continuous line of breakers which meant there were coral heads in our path. We couldn't get through. There wasn't a single gap in the reef large enough for even so small a boat as ours.

We were only about two miles from land, with the wind shoving us shoreward relentlessly, despite all the strength we put on the oars. The water was deep right up to the edge of the reef, so there was no hope of anchoring. For three hours, during the worst heat of the day, we struggled toward the nearest end of the island to the northwest. We rowed in desperation to get around the end of the island, but it was a losing battle.

The beach beyond the reef gradually filled with people who could only watch, unable to help. We were both naked, as was our usual habit in those temperatures. Once she caught sight of our audience on the beach, Sylvia wanted to dress, but she couldn't stop rowing. The coral loomed 30 yards from us, and there was still at least a mile to go before we could possibly row clear of it.

Then, to our shock, we realized that what we thought was the end of the island was only the point of a jutting reef. Even if we managed to clear the point, the reef went on beyond for another three miles.

A glance at Sylvia's face told me that she knew as well as I where the wind and currents were driving us. When you see those breakers and you're in a little boat about to get pitched against a coral wall, you know that it is certain death. It's like being in a head-on car collision at 80 miles an hour; you're finished.

The people on the shore watched silently. The strongest swimmers in the world cannot swim through coral heads as sharp as knives. The islanders never take their canoes to the weather side, because it's as dangerous to boat there as it is to swim. It never crossed my mind that *I* would soon be obliged to dive in for our one remaining chance to live.

We were still in deep water, although the bottom was visible now, rising abruptly about ten yards away. That gave us 20 yards to where the waves started to break—a scant safety zone. If the anchor grabbed and held right away . . . it was unlikely, but there was nothing better to try.

Sylvia was lashed to the boat, shaking. But she didn't panic. The size of the breakers was terrifying. They were shooting seven or eight feet higher than the other waves, and as they broke in curling foam we could see the jutting, brownish heads of coral, barely submerged, waiting to tear us apart. Add to it the deafening roar of a thousand breakers—then imagine the terror of a non-swimmer like Sylvia, and the guts it took for her to ride this out.

There was no hope for *Britannia II* to go through that and survive. My arms were two dead lumps. I had no strength left to grab the oars, let alone row the boat. I dropped the anchor overboard.

A few agonizing seconds went by. Suddenly we were in shallower water and the anchor held. I let out 30 feet of line. Just beyond us now, the first breakers rose like a menacing wall. They hit and began rocking us, sweeping us toward the coral. I secured the oars, pulled up the rudder and one of the two dagger boards that help stabilize the boat. The other dagger board was stuck; I couldn't have moved it even if I had wanted to. But that was not all bad, I reasoned; the dagger board might take the first bang and save *Britannia*'s bottom—for a while, at least.

We hit a coral head sideways, but not hard because the anchor was holding. I saw the people waving from the beach. Sylvia was putting on a swimsuit and I was yelling at her to stay in the boat, whatever happened. *Britannia* was unlikely to capsize, but if she did, Sylvia would be safer on board.

I had barely finished lifting the rudder when, with a lurch, the anchor chain snapped and *Britannia* was

drifting free again, *heading right for the reef.*
There was only one last desperate risk left. I remembered seeing a small gap between two coral heads, wide enough perhaps for *Britannia* to squeeze through. Beyond that it was shallow and the coral beneath seemed flat all the way to the beach. *Britannia* was lying broadside to shore. There was a momentary lull. I knew the next breaker was going to smash her against the reef unless I could point her into the gap, and there was only one way to do that in time.

I dove into the churning water, grabbed the bow and pushed to lead her into that one small opening. If luck wasn't with me, *Britannia* would smash me to a pulp against the reef.

People have asked me about religion. I depend more on luck. I believe luck will always come your way, but if you're not prepared to seize the advantage it will pass you by. Had I not been by nature and conditioning prepared to take immediate advantage of my luck, I don't think I would have been able to get *Britannia* in position for what happened next.

Exactly what happened I'll never know, because suddenly everything went dark. With a tremendous lurch the boat shot forward, sweeping me aside and under with such force that I lost my grip. It all happened in an instant. One moment I was pushing like a mad horse; the next I was in a maelstrom of foam and felt *Britannia* go over me like an express train. I was thrown flat against the coral bottom. When I managed to surface, I saw that the boat had been lifted through the gap and thrown over to lie on her side. Sylvia floundered in the water, pulling desperately on her lifeline to get back on board.

The only thing that kept *Britannia* from turning over was that there simply wasn't enough water under her. I closed the ten yards between us on the next breaker, which also righted the boat again. Sylvia was frantically trying to get free of her life-saving harness. I unhooked it for her and urged her on to the shore. Only the foam of the crashing breakers reached *Britannia* now, and though she was bouncing around in it she had taken all the damage she was going to.

It was like a dream. The Gilbertese came toward us, lifted Sylvia up and carried her ashore like a baby. Jabbering islanders surrounded me as I put on my trunks. Men, girls and children laughed, treating the whole affair as a huge lark. They helped drag *Britannia* into ankle-deep water, where I found her bottom staved in at two points.

Later, the island doctor invited us to live at his house until repairs could be made at the Tarawa shipyard, and he arranged for a shipping vessel to come from another island to tow us in. We had to empty the boat for the tow to Tarawa. Everything on board was filthy and soaked through. With the islanders' help, we salvaged what supplies we could. *Britannia* was not seaworthy enough for a tow until I did a patch-up repair with marine putty and scraps of wood.

The disaster left us in a stupor for weeks. We

laughed when we remembered *why* we had rowed into that near-fatal nightmare: to send a message that we were all right!

We shoved off from Onotoa on January 13th. Repairs at Tarawa were completed by February 7th, when we rowed the *Britannia* seaward once again. I was feeling lucky. And feeling lucky, I felt safe. Confident, too, as we came closer to success. Perhaps that is why I chanced tangling with a shark.

For some weeks I had been in the habit of going over the side to swim and spear fish. Then, on the 21st of March, a white-tip shark got me mad. He was small as sharks go, not five feet long, but the trouble he caused was considerable.

Had he been larger I would have used the speargun with the explosive head and promptly done away with him. But he was so small I didn't bother. I had noticed him hanging around earlier, but when I dove in for my daily swim he was nowhere to be seen, so I settled down to spear our dinner. I had speared two small fish when the white-tip reappeared. He was cheeky, and I had to poke his nose a few times with my spear to keep him at bay. He seemed to get the message and kept his distance as I hunted, but as soon as I speared my third small fish he came in and snatched it away. That did it. He wasn't going to get away with my catch!

I had been using barbless spears and thought it would be easy to pull out once I shot him. So I reloaded and shot him in the head. The spear went right through, but it wasn't a particularly good shot. Though stunned, the beast had plenty of fight left. I pulled and he pulled, but the spear wouldn't come out. I became so furious I closed in, grabbed him by his gills with one hand, his tail with the other, and kept him immobilized as I swam back to the boat. Once alongside, I yanked the spear free and passed the gun to Sylvia.

By then the shark's struggle was feeble, and I should have let it go at that. Instead, I asked Sylvia to pass me a sharp buck knife we kept for skinning fish, and then proceeded to rip his belly from mouth to tail. He began to thrash convulsively, and it was all I could do to hold on.

We went under fighting and drifted away. I was waiting for him to weaken before I let go and surfaced. Suddenly he broke away and turned on me, taking my right upper arm in his jaws. I felt a cold shock of pain. I grabbed behind his head with my left hand to pull him off and away. Once again he wriggled free, but instead of pressing the attack he slowly sank, as I surfaced.

I clamped my hand on my wound to stem the hemorrhage, and Sylvia helped me into the boat. Then mechanically, silently, she applied tetracycline to the wound and bandaged it.

Shock and despair set in. For the first time I felt we might not make it. We tried the radio and got not a bleep out of it. With Sylvia manning the oars—I couldn't possibly row—we attempted to reach New Caledonia, 200 miles away, but failed due to a change in the wind.

Now our only hope was for a ship to sight us. We saw two, and one passed only two miles from us—yet despite our use of smoke flares and parachute star shells, they sailed by.

My arm throbbed painfully. I feared gangrene. Shark bites are notoriously infectious, and we had scant medical knowledge for an injury as severe as mine. The wound measured about six by two inches. The flesh was chewed down to the muscle layer which, while undamaged, was completely exposed. The thought of gangrene became an obsession. We were keeping a 24-hour watch for ships, but had no luck. To double our misery, the barometer fell and the weather worsened. This was our introduction to "Emily," the cyclone into which we were later reported to have vanished.

My log entry for the last days of March tells the story: *Barometer down 4 milbars. Continuous rain. Total overcast. Sea is ten feet. Wind 15 to 20 miles per hour. Brampton Reefs probably 100 miles west of us. Present position uncertain. Afraid we're in for something.* Britannia *battened down, rigged for worst. Keeping our fingers crossed. . . . Barometer low. Feel cyclone around. Ghastly weather. Wind 30 knots. Drifting. Tiller broke. Fearing shipwreck reefs any minute. Arm hurts bad. Rain.* Britannia *swamped often. Having bad time all around.*

Poor Sylvia worked on alone. She had to sit on the gunwales to right the boat after each swamping. She reloaded things that came loose, and had to bale by herself. I slipped into delirium, and for days, as we skirted the edge of Cyclone Emily, I dreamed.

Despite my strange, feverlike drift of mind there was no sign of gangrene. My wound seemed to be healing. It was painful to hold the sextant, so I didn't take sights often and had no precise idea where we were. We heard on the receiver that a cyclone coming from the sea had struck the Australian coast around Goadstone. My luck had steered us safely distant from its center.

Yet something was wrong, missing. We soon realized what it was: the absence of our Mexican flies. Apparently they had died. "Of what?" Sylvia asked.

I replied, "Of boredom!" Her laughter was heartier than I expected.

On the 5th of April, 1972—almost a year out of San Francisco—we heard on the transistor that we were "Notice Number 13": *"All ships in the Coral Sea requested to keep a strict lookout for the rowboat* Britannia II *and inform of position and condition of occupants John Fairfax and Sylvia Cook."*

We sighted a ship that same day. It passed 500 yards from us. Nobody saw us. So much for the strict lookout.

Had we been sighted, we would merely have had the ship send a message that we were still afloat and proceeding more or less on course. We were so near our goal that the idea of being picked up depressed us both. Yet later there were times when my arm hurt so intensely I would have been willing to throw in the towel. Next day I wouldn't hear of it.

Vacillating that way, we progressed by wind and current until, with *Britannia* practically empty, our supplies and water almost gone, we came to the Great Barrier Reef.

We were worried stiff. The Australian coast is only partially charted. The weather was horrible. We were swamped continuously, and life was sheer misery. Sylvia couldn't row much under those conditions and, drifting, we were faced with a 50-percent possibility of smashing up as we did at Onotoa—or worse.

Pushed by 20- to 25-mile winds, we swept across one of the foulest stretches of reef water I have ever seen—miraculously without a scratch. Exhausted, we slept, only to wake up surrounded by enormous breakers. Steering cautiously, we rowed across this shoal ground looking for an anchorage, and after some hair-raising progress found a patch of sand four fathoms deep.

At anchor, I began tinkering with the radio generator and batteries, because we were once again in a hell of a spot. That part of the Barrier Reef had not been surveyed; the reefs weren't marked on the chart. It was doubtful any skipper would bring his boat out to tow us. We'd have to try to make it on our own—a desperate necessity almost guaranteed to end in disaster.

Log entry, April 16: *Tried the radio last night but no luck. By using the transistor we discovered that we are* transmitting (on the Marconi) and by activating the SARBE [Search and Rescue Beacon Equipment for beaming distress signals to passing planes] that we are not receiving (on the Marconi). However, our transmission must be extremely weak as we only have one battery serviceable and nobody seems to have picked us up . . . If this reef is uncharted it means that nobody ever comes here, which means it's a hell of a place for us to be. If we are wrecked we'll rot and nobody will ever find out . . . Can see clearly the reef barrier and rocks that surround us in a semi-circle from NE to SW.

The action of tide and wind shifted *Britannia II* from side to side in a wide arc. Our anchor cable was by then badly rusted. It had been rubbing against submerged coral heads and was bound to break at any time. Normally I would have dived at intervals to keep it clear, but the condition of my arm prevented that. And so, in the middle of the night, after three days at anchor, we found ourselves adrift—and with no anchor this time to stop us short of the reef.

For the next three days we slept only briefly, one at a time. The mere thought of night was terrifying. In the dark we could hear the occasional roar of breaking waves and the characteristic rustle of tidal rips that whirled *Britannia* around like a toy. Hope of survival in these waters was so low that neither of us gave another thought to my arm. It was a seaman's nightmare.

But once again, our luck saw us through—luck plus some careful navigation. By alternately drifting and rowing for three days and nights, we made it in over the Great Barrier Reef—the final obstacle to our conquest of the Pacific.

After 361 days and 8,000 miles of open water, our goal was at last in sight.

We could see land. *Australia!*

Ordeal in the Yukon

BY HELEN KLABEN WITH BETH DAY

8

In mid-winter, 1963, a 21-year-old Brooklyn girl named Helen Klaben hitched a ride in a light, antiquated plane flying from Fairbanks, Alaska, to San Francisco. It crashed in the wilderness—and she, along with the pilot, 40-year-old Ralph Flores, faced a 49-day ordeal of staggering proportions.

Miss Klaben's arm was broken, and her foot seriously slashed. Ralph's injuries were even more painful: a broken jaw, cracked ribs, jagged facial cuts.

They had no survival gear—no axe, no bandages, no emergency rations—and in a little more than a week ate all their food. From then on they lived on melted snow—sometimes flavored with a little toothpaste.

After more than a month at the crash site, they decided their only hope for rescue was for Ralph to walk out, seeking a trapper's cabin or a settlement, or at least a clearing from which to signal a plane. Helen was in no condition to travel, so she was left to fend for herself. . . .

• The day after Ralph left, the temperature dropped, the wind started howling through the trees, and there were snow flurries. I worried about Ralph. He had only his parka and my coat for cover and warmth. I was afraid he would freeze to death.

My legs were terribly cold. I decided to borrow a pair of Ralph's trousers. They were in one of his trunks that he had taken outside the plane and placed against the fuselage. To my surprise and bewilderment, I found the trunk locked. Ralph must have locked it just before leaving. His other trunk—the one with all his religious books—he had left unlocked. I brooded for a while about this strange quirk of Ralph's and then decided to forget about it, since there wasn't anything I could do about it anyway.

That was one of the few times I ventured outside the plane for the next week. I realized that because of the bad weather no planes would be likely to stray over me or my signal fire. Before he'd left, Ralph had always been the one to make the fires. He had taught me how to do it the last few days. Although Ralph had said he was going to leave me plenty of wood, in the end he cut up only enough for what I calculated might last three days—the minimum time he'd said he would be gone. There was also a pile of green pine for smoke signals in case I ever did hear a plane. I don't know what I did wrong, but I couldn't make the fire work well. Some of the wood burned nicely, but most of it seemed to smoke a lot, and smell. If I got close enough to get warm, the smoke blew in my eyes and the fumes made me cough.

So I stayed inside most of the time. It did not take me long to realize I was warmer than when Ralph had been with me. The crude sleeping blanket I had made from the plane's insulation and carpeting was very snug. If only we had thought of it before, we would have saved ourselves from all those miserable nights.

I think the worst thing about my being alone was time. My watch had been broken in the crash. Ralph had let me wear his self-winding wrist watch occasionally when we were together, but I wore it on my broken arm and didn't move it enough to keep it wound. Naturally, Ralph took his watch with him when he left. He gave me the clock from the plane, which had also broken in the crash, but which he had repaired. The clock stopped the day after Ralph left. I tried to make it run by shaking it and standing it on its head, but it never gave even one encouraging tick. It was dead.

So I had no way of telling time. That first day was cloudy, and it was impossible for me to tell if it was 2 P.M., 4 P.M. or 5 P.M. Should I try to sleep now? I wondered. Or should I read a few more hours? It was like living in the Twilight Zone. Just the gray, timeless nothingness.

March 8, the day after Ralph left, one month and four days after we'd crashed, I started to keep a sort of diary—in the form of a letter to my family.

"To all my loved ones, especially my dearest, most wonderful mother:

"It's been over a month since I left Fairbanks—or civilization," I began. "I am sitting in the plane somewhere in the Yukon or perhaps British Columbia writing this testimonial. I waited this long hoping to be able to write it at home. Now I'm sorry I didn't write this adventure as a daily log.

"There is so much I want to say. So much we've learned. My foremost desire is to be home with you now. And with the mercy of our most generous Lord I will be soon, I pray."

I went on for a page or so, describing my decision to make the trip, my meeting with Ralph, finally taking off. . . . But when I came to the crash, I couldn't go any further. The whole thing sounded too much like an epitaph, and I quit. There's no point writing the end, I told myself, till the end has come. I stayed burrowed in the blanket, hoping Ralph had found some way to protect himself.

So long as it snowed I knew no planes would come over. I decided to let the fire go out and just stay inside the plane, covered up in the blanket, and read away the time. I boiled enough water to last a few days—but it froze. I also put one of the oil cans at hand to use as a urinal. Then I settled into my insulated blanket, with my books at hand, my conveniences close by, to wait out the storm—and Ralph's return.

By now the bandage on my arm had gotten unraveled, and I had always felt it was too tight, anyway, so I undid the whole thing. My arm, when I had it unwrapped, looked so white and skinny and yet swollen from the tight wrapping. I put the splints back on and rebound it loosely so my arm could breathe. It felt better.

Since I had privacy, I examined my body more closely. I hadn't known I had cuts on my legs until they began to itch a week after we crashed. Now they all seemed to be healing nicely, with only a few half-moon scars on my leg and knee and ankle. I unbandaged my feet and bathed them. They always hurt more after they had been bathed, but I felt they should be kept as clean as possible. The blisters on my heel were more or less the same, but the lower section of my right foot seemed to have worsened. Underneath the black crust the flesh seemed to be disintegrating. I could see the outline of the bones. My foot smelled as if it were rotting away, so I quickly wrapped it up again. I suppose I should have been scared, but I wasn't.

It was a trial to know what to do with my feet now. When I put them down they throbbed. Yet it was difficult to keep them up, particularly in the plane, where the angle was awkward. I still thought my foot and toes were alive because of the intensity of the stabbing pains, which I assumed was blood circulating. I kept imagining what would happen when I was rescued, and I visualized my foot in a whirlpool bath.

My dirty condition was bothering me by now, too. My hair was grimy and smelled and my scalp itched all the time, especially at night when I was chilled and restless. When I couldn't stand it any longer, I'd finally get one hand out from under the covers and slip it under my hood and scratch.

Yet your body at a time like that becomes curiously removed from yourself. It is an outer thing you care for and contemplate objectively. Things have happened to it and are happening to it, but it's almost as though your body belonged to someone else. The worse the things that happen to your body the more you tend to withdraw into yourself. Eventually you feel like a small inner core surrounded by a physical problem that you cope with as best you can. After a while, it doesn't even concern you very much. You are you: the creature inside, busy with your thoughts and dreams. When the body intrudes, you treat it as a kindly nurse would, then go back to your own inner self again.

The weather at the crash site continued bad, but at least the blizzard had stopped. The three days Ralph had expected to be gone came and passed. And then four . . . and five. I didn't really worry. If Ralph had survived the blizzard—and somehow I felt he had—then he might have found the highway he'd thought he'd seen, and started walking toward civilization. If he was alive, he'd be back for me. If he didn't come back? Well, if it ever got warm again, I thought I'd bundle my feet as best I could, and try to follow his tracks, if the snow hadn't erased them all. It still didn't really occur to me that I might die, that I might freeze, that I might be starving to death.

Once, when the wind came and blew the snow away for a few hours, I ventured outside. I was inching around, looking things over, guiding my steps by holding on to the plane, when my hand hit something on top of the fuselage that made me pause and look. It was a wad of chewing gum. I clawed it off the plane and popped it into my mouth. Our chewing-gum supply had run out long ago. But when I'd finished mine, I'd thrown it away. Frugal Ralph had stored his for the future. It was frozen hard, but after I gnawed at it a few minutes it began to melt. I felt as elated as though I'd just discovered a frozen five course TV dinner. I didn't think Ralph would mind my using his gum.

It was about 3 P.M. of the eighth day I had been alone. Another gray, depressing day in which I'd stayed wrapped in my blanket inside the plane. I had not even bothered to try and melt some water for the last two days. When I had prayed that morning, I had asked God for "just a little miracle. Not a big one, Lord. Just a little one"; that He be with Ralph and protect him. Not for me, but for our families.

Now I was reading the Bible Ralph had left me. Suddenly I sat up, thinking I had heard an odd sound, like a call. I listened, then went back to the Bible. My ears were so bad now that I could hear little. Then I stopped reading again; I *had* heard something. I threw back the tarpaulin that covered the door, and listened, my head outside the plane.

It was a cry. "Helen!" Ralph's voice. Far off in the woods.

I started to jump out of the plane and go to him. Then I stopped, remembering how he'd fuss at me for getting my sore feet filled with snow. I made myself sit back and wait, crying with relief. It was nearly a half hour later when Ralph trudged into the clearing.

I was so happy I jumped out of the plane and hugged and kissed him, laughing and crying all at the same time. My "little miracle" had been answered.

Ralph had worked his way downhill from our mountainside and found a clearing he felt would make a good campsite. He had made a shelter for us there, and then waited, hoping a plane would sight him. But no plane ever appeared, so he decided to come back for me, after first exploring the lake. Ralph wanted us to move down to the clearing, where our camp would be more visible from the air, before he tried to go on farther and follow the sound.

It snowed all day on March 16, the day after Ralph returned, but we kept busy, preparing for our trip, anyway. When I showed Ralph the little clock that had let me down, he fixed it within a few minutes. He made a toboggan out of part of the fuselage and a piece of spruce. We decided to take the cushions from the plane, the sleeping bag I'd made, a strip of fabric with the plane's identification number, engine cover, coats, cans, clothes. Ralph had two metal suitcases but decided they were too heavy. Instead, we filled my fabric dress bag with sweaters and coats. As I had lost weight, and my clothes fell more slackly on my body, letting in air drafts, I had added more clothes to keep warm. By now I was wearing four pairs of pants—two of my own and two I had wheedled out of Ralph—and four sweaters. Ralph thought my camera was too heavy to bother with, but I took it anyway, since it belonged to my sister. I took my make-up case and Ralph his shaving kit, since we both wanted to look our best when we got home.

I was supposed to sit on the back of the loaded toboggan, since I had no snowshoes, but when we had it piled high and I sat on it, it was far too heavy either to pull or push. I got off, and it was still immovable. Ralph cut the toboggan in half, and we reloaded, leaving much of our original load behind.

We were finally ready to leave around 3 P.M. on what I thought was March 17, but I have since reconstructed my chronology and learned that often I was one or two days off. Anyway, it had stopped snowing, though the skies had not cleared and it was bitterly cold. The last thing I did before leaving the site was paint a directional sign on the plane. The sign, painted with my red oil paints, was to direct anyone who might find the plane before they found us.

WENT
→
2 MI.
DOWN HILL
3/16/63

Since Ralph could not pull me on the sled, he fixed my feet for walking by wrapping them with extra canvas, which he roped to my legs. He put me in front, with a rope over my good shoulder, to steer the sled. Ralph pushed from behind.

He told me to walk in his old tracks that he had made coming back to the plane. I tried, but it had snowed since then and half the time I fell through. Once I got started I could keep my feet moving, but if anything stopped me I found I could not pick up my right foot. Ralph had to come around to the front and lift it for me. Then I could move forward again till I went through the snow or stumbled. Each time my foot went down in the deep snow the ropes that held the canvas came undone. With only one functioning arm, it was impossible for me to retie them. Ralph had to come and tie them for me, then get me started again.

He wasn't in much better shape than I was. Our load was simply too heavy to pull wearing snowshoes, so Ralph took them off, piled them on top of the sled, and floundered in and out of drifts as I was doing, falling almost as often.

We couldn't synchronize our movements. When Ralph gave a push from the back, the momentum caused me to fall forward, sometimes to my knees. Our trail led us through deep snow, in and out of steep gullies full of brush, trees, windfall logs. Even with good feet to walk on, it would have been murderous.

I tasted bile in my mouth and felt as though I might vomit. I wanted to sink down in the snow and just rest and get my breath back, but I couldn't keep Ralph waiting. Finally we came to a dead stop midway up a small, steep hill when I fell down and the toboggan went over with me. Ralph—ever patient, determined, steady—decided it was not balanced properly, so he took everything off, got it reloaded, then reroped it, while I sat in the snow gasping.

We hit another hill so steep I would not have tried to ski down it. I couldn't help Ralph with the weight; the most I could do was steer a little with the lead rope over my good shoulder. We got up somehow but, going downhill, Ralph expected me to go ahead and guide the sled. I couldn't. I didn't have enough balance to hold myself, let alone the sled. I tried to walk down —and fell end over end, rolling the length of the hill. If I were in New York in Central Park, I thought, I'd call this fun.

When my body stopped turning, I looked back and saw Ralph coming down fast, around bushes and trees, trying to brake the toboggan from behind so it wouldn't run away from him. I hated myself for not being able to help him, but I could hardly help myself. I couldn't recall ever experiencing such agonizing exhaustion.

It took us five hours to make the run of "about two miles" that was actually, I later learned, less than three-quarters of one mile. The last fifty yards in failing light—uphill to a knoll—were the worst. Now Ralph was pulling the sled and I was trying to push, but I had no leverage in the deep snow. The only thing I could push with was my belly. I thrust it against the sled and pushed with all the strength I could summon. The sled went a little way, then stopped. We couldn't get it moving again.

Ralph decided to take some of our things off the toboggan and carry them up the hill to the campsite in the clearing. It was dark now, and he was soon out of sight. I just sank down in the snow, waiting for him to come back. The canvases had slipped off my feet and I couldn't retie them. I couldn't go on. I knew if Ralph didn't come back for me, I would never get up again.

Ralph did come back, and told me to follow right behind him. We both carried some more stuff from the toboggan. When we finally got to the top of the knoll, I slipped down to the ground and just lay there. I couldn't move; I couldn't breathe. My mind was still clear but my body was gone. I watched Ralph push away the snow from the lean-to he'd built before when he was living in the clearing, feeling guilty that I was just lying there when there was so much work to do. I wanted water in the most terrible way, yet I didn't want to ask him to stop and fix it.

Then I began to throw up. There was nothing in my stomach—except its own secretions. There was bile, a terrible, thick, green, vile-tasting fluid that ran from the corners of my mouth. When he heard me retching, Ralph stopped his work and came over to me and held my head.

He had not wanted to build a fire because the firelight would blot out our faint trail marks in the dark, and he had to make other trips back to the toboggan. Now he made one quick trip back, then got a fire going, boiled water and brought me some. Nothing in my life ever tasted so good. The next thing Ralph did was to take the soaked sweaters off my feet and dry them over the fire. He bound my feet with rags torn out of one of my cotton nightgowns we'd taken along on the toboggan for just that purpose.

All this revived me somewhat; enough, anyway, to enable me to help him fix up our shelter for the night. Moving very slowly, we stretched a tarpaulin on the ground, placed the cushions and blanket on top of that, and settled in. It was about 11:30 P.M.

The next morning it was cloudy but not snowing. Ralph staggered off down the slope and hauled the toboggan back up to our clearing. Then he got his hammer and chisel out of his toolbox and started hacking away at the trees again. For two days Ralph worked, cutting up a wood supply for the fire and improving our shelter. He used the toboggan standing on its end as one wall and wired it together with poles and limbs. Over the top and along the sides Ralph hung pieces of canvas and wired and roped these to a crossbar and to the poles. We made a crude sort of floor out of some more limbs and on top of these we placed a lot of spruce boughs. As I watched Ralph labor away, it suddenly occurred to me that he'd had nothing to eat for —I counted up—over thirty days. Even then, his strength and endurance seemed unbelievable.

While we worked Ralph told me that, as soon as he was rested from our trek, he was going on down to the beaver lake he had found, and make an S.O.S. in the snow in the meadow beside it, since bush pilots always look at the water markers along their routes. Then, he said, he would go on toward the engine-like sound we'd been hearing in the distance.

I seemed to have left my feeling of safety and comfort at the wrecked plane. There was something eerie about this place that made me uneasy. I looked around at the charred black fingers of the trees and the bleak white snow. There was nothing alive.

"I saw tracks of large animals on the way here," I told Ralph.

"Probably just a bunch of rabbits."

"No, they were big paw marks. Much bigger than a rabbit's." I looked at him, not wanting to plead, but I was afraid. "I don't want to be alone here."

"It won't be for long," he said. "You'll be safe with a big fire going. Even if there are large animals, they won't come up to the fire. I've got to get on down there and make that signal where it's sure to be seen."

Ralph looked off toward the lake, his eyes fixed in their private plan. I realized it was for the best.

I wondered if he was really strong enough to go on. He had visibly wasted since he first left me. His once-stocky body was now a skinny frame on which the conglomeration of sweaters and jackets hung loosely. His face was thin and sunken; the eye above the injured cheekbone had a wild look.

"Yes, but first you must rest," I said finally.

"I'll rest today," he said. "It's too cloudy to go on. But if the weather is all right tomorrow, I'll leave."

The rest of that day Ralph spent gathering enough wood to last me for two days. But for hours, on and off, he was seized by violent attacks of abdominal cramps that left him doubled up in the snow. I had never seen Ralph cry before, but now I watched him stop chiseling wood when the spasms attacked him, and stand there, his arms around his belly, tears streaking down through the dirt and stubble on his face. He had held me when I vomited. I tried to think of something I could do for him. In the end, I started reading the Bible aloud to him while he clutched himself.

That afternoon I sat by the fire and unbandaged my feet. I knew the trip had aggravated them, possibly stirred up a new infection. I found both feet were running a mucuslike fluid and they had that terrible smell now. I could see clearly the ends of bone protruding through the black crust of the right foot. I held it up and showed it to Ralph. "Do you think I'll lose my toes?" I asked him. "Do you think my toes will fall off?" I wasn't thinking of possible surgical amputation. I just thought if they really died completely, they'd drop off my foot, like overripe fruit.

"No," Ralph said. "They'll be all right, daughter. They won't fall off."

"Okay, Daddy-O, if you say so."

I tore up fresh bandages and tied up my feet, so we could both forget about them.

When the next day dawned clear, I knew Ralph would leave, regardless of anything I might say. He had the look in his eye of a man absolutely possessed. It was as if he were deliberately spending his last measure of strength—or perhaps summoning a strength he didn't have himself but that was inspired.

I didn't say any more about not wanting to be left

alone. I'd got along before. I would have to make my own peace again.

Then we heard the noise around noon. It sounded closer from here. To Ralph it was a good omen. He strapped on his snowshoes, tied his pack on his back, put the binoculars around his neck, and took the compass and his spear in his hands. Then, with my silly hat still on his head, he started out once more.

Again I sat by the fire, watching and calling after him, my eyes misted with tears. He was so weak now.

It was, I thought, March 20. I wrote in my notebook. "Ralph left . . . please, God, be with him."

Ralph's second expedition was successful. He wrote an S.O.S. in the snow in letters 70 feet high near the lake and added a huge arrow that pointed to the camp where Helen was waiting. Four days later, the S.O.S. was spotted by a bush pilot.

When the first rescuer arrived, Helen Klaben began to cry. "After forty-nine days," she wrote, "I just sort of let go."

Bail-Out at Supersonic Speed

BY ARTHUR RAY HAWKINS WITH WESLEY PRICE

9

Lieutenant Commander Arthur Ray Hawkins, one of the Navy's most decorated pilots (in World War II he shot down 14 enemy planes before he was old enough to vote), was the first human being to be ejected from a disabled plane traveling faster than the speed of sound. It happened 40,000 feet over Mississippi. That he escaped the plane at all was the first miracle; that he didn't die from lack of oxygen was the second. Here is his story.

• I've never been more scared or nearer to death than I was one summer a number of years ago on a routine flight from New York to Texas. I had this jet fighter at 40,000 feet, cruising level. It was so safe, so easy; and then, over Mississippi, the plane went crazily supersonic and tried to kill me.

At that time I was doing a lot of acrobatic flying with the Navy's air-show team, the Blue Angels. I was leader. There were six of us, and we were all together, flying in line abreast, when my plane went out of control. It dived into an enormous outside loop—I was vertical—then I was upside down, hanging by my safety belt, and beginning to red out as centrifugal force whirled blood into my brain. That would terrify any man, especially when you know you're traveling faster than the speed of sound. If I was going to bail out, I'd have to go now, before I lost consciousness—now or never. But the slipstream outside my canopy was supersonic; plunging into those granite-hard shock waves might smash the life out of me. In all the history of aviation, no one had pierced the sonic wall with his unarmored body. At least, no one had survived to tell about it.

I remember thinking of all that; at the same time, I felt sorry that my airplane was going to auger in and be destroyed. It was an F9F-6 Cougar, the last word in Grumman-built Navy fighters—wings swept back, lots of fizz out the rear end, and a red-line speed above Mach 1. ["Mach" numbers indicate the ratio of a plane's speed to the speed of sound at the temperature at which a plane is flying; the speed of sound varies according to temperature.]

It all started when six of us flew north from our base at Corpus Christi, Texas, to pick up the first shipment of the new plane. We arrived in Bethpage, New York, late in the day, and the next day swarmed into the Grumman factory, six eager guys. We tried out the plane on a quick training flight and finished the hop well satisfied. Then we took off for home.

On the way we stopped at Sewart Air Force Base in Smyrna, Tennessee, for fuel and lunch. So far, so good. Leaving Smyrna, it took us about twenty minutes to get climbed out and formed in line abreast. We weren't pushing our engines, but another hour would see us in Corpus Christi.

Or so I thought. I had no premonition of danger. The controls felt a little sloppy, but that's natural at 40,000 feet. A normal stick movement isn't enough in skinny air. And then you move the stick big, and it's too much, and you get into a loop. But nothing to worry about.

I turned my head left, and right, to see the other jets. When I looked forward again, my nose had dropped a little below the horizon. That's no worry either. You ease back on the stick slightly, the nose rises, and there you are. But this time there was no response to stick movement. The nose stayed down. Then it went farther down.

I thought I could recover by adjusting the elevator trim tab. It was already set a little nose-up, just enough for level cruise at altitude. I thumbed the button on my stick, feeding in more nose-up trim. Not too much.

But the dive steepened. My air speed was getting very high. I fed in more trim tab. No response. More trim tab, and more, until I had all of it—15 degrees. Still no response; the airplane was getting away from me, diving steeper and steeper, building up speed every moment. I heard one of the boys call on the radio, "There goes Hawk; he's in trouble!"

Centrifugal force was pulling me out of my seat, and I realized I was in the first arc of an outside loop. What had gone wrong? I had only seconds left to figure this out.

Not the trim tab. Might be the flying tail, switched on accidentally. No, the switch is still at Off position. The engine, then, a sudden flame-out . . . but the gauge shows I'm pulling 90 percent power . . . of course it might be stuck there—

To test instrument response, I shoved the throttle forward. The gauge went to 95 percent; so power wasn't my trouble. The dive angle was now about 35 degrees, and my speed was approaching a dangerous level. Machmeter and air-speed needles were wheeling around together. I cut my power, dropped the dive brakes and went to my emergency trim-tab system, flicking the switch with my left hand. It had no effect.

Another glance at the instrument panel showed that I was already past the speed of sound—and the needles were still winding up. Dive angle 50 degrees . . .

Vertical! The loop's centrifugal force had me pinned up against the canopy, and a crimson haze began to cloud my vision. It was the first stage of a red-out. There was one last hope—keep pressure on the stick, full nose-up trim, and switch on the flying tail.

I flipped the switch. With that, the airplane tucked under, and I was upside down, hanging in my harness. Vision was going; consciousness would go next. There was just enough time left to jettison the plastic canopy and fire the explosive charge that would cannon me into space, seat and all. I knew the bail-out drill by heart:

Depress this lever; it blows off the canopy and arms the explosive shell behind your seat. Draw your feet back into the stirrups. Reach overhead; grasp two handles and pull the protective curtain over your face. The last inch of pull will trigger a firing pin. Boom! Out you go.

But I couldn't get the sequence started. Hung up in the canopy as I was, my reach wasn't long enough to shove down the first lever. Stretching to the utmost, I could just graze it with a fingertip.

One last chance. Alongside my head was an emergency handle to be used only in desperate cases. It would arm the ejection seat. But it wouldn't blow off the canopy. To get out of this supersonic mantrap, I'd have to fire myself through thick plastic glass.

I pulled the handle.

How tough is my helmet? Duck down. Maybe the seat rails will punch a hole for you.

I pulled down the face curtain.

When the ejection charge fired, I was four or five inches off the seat. It came up and hit me like a pile driver. Too stunned to feel anything, I went through the canopy, a limp bundle traveling faster than sound. When the momentary blackout passed, I found myself clawing for my rip cord in a groggy attempt to open my parachute. Then I saw that I had missed the handle, and torn a pocket from my flight suit.

Then I thought, *How stupid! Wait until you slow down. A chute opened at this speed would be torn to shreds.*

The seat and I were tumbling over and over, but that soon stopped, and I was sitting upright in space, falling with a lot of forward motion, like an artillery shell. It was then that I realized I was bareheaded. The wind had torn away my face curtain, helmet and oxygen mask.

No oxygen, altitude still above 30,000 feet—I'd gasp my life out if I opened the parachute and dangled up here. I decided to fall free, two or three miles, to get into breathable air as soon as possible. So I fell, keeping one hand on the trip that would jettison my seat, and the other on the rip-cord handle.

Two or three miles? Why, in about four seconds the lack of oxygen was graying me out. If I blacked out entirely, I knew that I might never wake up in time to pop the chute.

At an altitude later estimated as 29,000 feet, I opened my safety belt and pulled the rip cord. When the chute blossomed, It jerked the living fool out of me. The shock was so great that I thought the canopy had torn, but looking up, I saw it was intact.

Next, I thought of my feet and legs. As far as I knew, I was the first Navy pilot to be fired through a canopy. But a lot of dummies had been shot through in experiments, and I'd read the reports: most of them had feet torn off, legs shattered, heads bashed in. My head

felt all right, and I saw that my feet were still attached to my legs.

The ground below was so far away that it didn't seem to be coming up at all. The only sound was a soft whistling of air in my parachute. And then I couldn't see the ground, or the parachute, or anything. My vision faded away, and I seemed to be suspended in gray fog. I needed oxygen.

After a while, I heard a jet go by. I was too grayed out to see it, but I knew it was one of the Blue Angels, following me down. I could think, after a fashion, and hear, and feel—I remember feeling the intense cold. But I couldn't see. Then, finally, the blackout. I came back to gray; sank into blackness once more; again regained gray consciousness. The blackouts scared me. If I could only hang on until I got down where there was oxygen pressure!

The chute drifted down through a layer of rough air that swung me from side to side. I was violently sick. Afterward, I felt better. My vision cleared, and in a space of mental clarity I remember a lesson from Navy flight training, about "grunt breathing."

"If you lose your oxygen mask in a high-altitude bailout," we were told, "take deep breaths, close your mouth and grunt hard. That will put pressure on the air in your lungs, and force oxygen into your bloodstream."

I tried it, inhaling, holding it and straining to put on pressure. Pressure is the thing; there's oxygen at high altitude, but it's at low pressure. A few seconds after each grunt, my vision would improve for a while. Now I could see the jet. The pilot was flying figure eights to stay with me, but keeping a safe distance so his jet blast wouldn't collapse my chute.

I learned later that my plane completed only the first half of its outside loop. After it got on its back, it went down at a steep angle, augered in and exploded. One of the other Blue Angels followed it down—when he leveled out he was barely 500 feet off the ground—and saw the plane strike in a wooded area, doing no harm.

Two of the other flyers and I met at 22,000 feet. One stayed up there, feeding radio reports to the nearest military air base, while the other flew descending figure eights alongside me. It was a long, slow drop, and everybody was getting low on fuel.

The entire accident, including the slow float down, took about half an hour. It seemed even longer to me, hanging in the chute. I wanted to give a wave, to let the pilot know I was alive, but being starved for oxygen, I lacked the strength to lift an arm.

Grunt breathing kept me alive all the way down to 10,000 feet, and there I could breathe normally. At 5,000 feet, I was able to raise my arms in a semaphore *R*. The *R* stood for "Roger"—O.K. The ground was coming up fast—woods, cotton patches, highways. I was drifting toward a country road, and I could see a pickup truck moving to intercept me. People sitting in the back were looking up at me; I counted two men, a woman and three children.

I missed a barbwire fence and landed in a cotton

patch. The chute quietly collapsed on the ground. People from the truck came running. I felt too weak to get up right away.

One of the men said, "Shall I help you up? I might fall down helping you. I'm scareder than you are."

I told him to let me sit awhile. One of the planes buzzed us. Since I didn't feel like getting up just yet, I asked one of the men—Mr. Arthur Edwards, a farmer and ex-deputy sheriff—to signal for me. "Wave to him on the next pass, so he'll know I'm all right."

Back came the jet, shrieking, and Mr. Edwards waved his hat. That didn't satisfy the pilot; he could see me sitting up, but I didn't look very lively. He came by again at 100 feet. I got on my feet, semaphoring "Roger" and a wave-off. He waggled his wings, and with drying tanks, went off on a beeline for NAS Memphis.

Mr. Edwards told me I was in Mississippi, near the town of Pickens. Then he drove me to the scene of the crash, about three miles away. A rising column of smoke led us to a wooded area, where a crowd of farm people were standing around a deep crater. Fire smoldered in the pit my plane had dug, and chunks of metal were scattered everywhere.

Mr. Edwards then drove me into Pickens, where I put in a long-distance call to my wife. She'd be waiting now, knowing I was overdue.

When she came on the phone, she was crying, and I told her if she didn't hush up, I couldn't tell her anything. It was awful, hearing her cry; she never cries. I assured her that I was all right. She wasn't satisfied with that. She knew I had bailed out. I told her that one of my ribs was slightly out of kilter, but other than that, I was fine.

"Where are you calling from—a hospital?"

"A drugstore," I said; and I kidded her a little to let her be really sure everything was all right. She stopped crying.

It was after dark when I landed at the Naval Air Station in Memphis. The other pilots were waiting for me, and there was an ambulance I didn't need. But I had to go to the Navy hospital, willy-nilly, where they looked me over—I had nothing worse than this one rib—and told me to return in the morning for X rays. For a man who had been through a supersonic bailout, an unheard-of thing, I was in good shape. For instance, I might have frozen to death, floating so long in subzero temperatures at high altitude. Luckily, the slipstream hadn't torn off my shoes or gloves, and I was wearing my uniform under the flight suit. Only my ears were slightly frostbitten.

After X rays the next day, I was flown back to Corpus Christi. I came stumbling off the transport plane, and there were all these people waiting—my wife with our boys, and a dozen of my best friends, and a few officials—a very happy reunion.

But my wife had tears in her eyes, and later on she said to me, "I'm never going to worry again. The Lord is saving you for something; you better start listening to find out what it is."

About the Compiler/Editor

Robert Gannon is a free-lance writer specializing in scientific subject for the general reader. His book for young readers, *What's Under a Rock?* explores the miniature world of animals and plants to be found there.

As adventures editor of *Popular Science* magazine, Mr. Gannon has become an adventurer in his own right. He has flown through a hurricane, dived to the bottom of the sea, climbed a mountain and even tried to ride a unicycle, reporting his experiences for the magazine.

Mr. Gannon lives in Tillson, New York.